**EDUCATING FOR
PURPOSEFUL LIFE**

EDUCATING FOR PURPOSEFUL LIFE

A NEW CONCEPTION OF SCHOOLING FOR THE 21ST CENTURY

S. David Brazer
Michael B. Matsuda

HARVARD EDUCATION PRESS
CAMBRIDGE, MA

Copyright © 2023 by the President and Fellows of Harvard College

All material relating to AUHSD used with permission of Anaheim Union High School District.

All rights reserved. No part of this publication may be reproduced or transmitted in any form or by any means, electronic or mechanical, including photocopy, recording, or any information storage and retrieval systems, without permission in writing from the publisher.

Paperback ISBN 978-1-68253-858-6

Library of Congress Cataloging-in-Publication Data is on file.

Published by Harvard Education Press,
an imprint of the Harvard Education Publishing Group

Harvard Education Press
8 Story Street
Cambridge, MA 02138

Cover Design: Ciano Design
Cover Image: Dimitris66/DigitalVision Vectors via Getty Images

The typefaces in this book are Adobe Garamond Pro and Futura PT.

CONTENTS

Foreword   ix

Introduction   1
1. Changing the Narrative   7
2. Generating Positive Change with Systems Thinking   27
3. Addressing Every Student's Story, Fostering Agency   61
4. Building a Network to Elevate Youth Voice and Purpose   79
5. Mindfulness and the Fifth C   117
6. Teacher Professional Learning   129
7. The Promise of the Career Preparedness Systems Framework   147
    Appendix A: Additional Sources of Support for the CPSF   163
    Appendix B: Programs That Support the CPSF   167

Notes   169
Acknowledgments   179
About the Authors   181
Index   183

We dedicate this book to the school board members, educators, students, parents, and community partners of the Anaheim Union High School District. They walk hand in hand toward purposeful life, a stronger community, and a better world.

FOREWORD

The Graphic and Comprehensive Nature
of Systemic Change in Action

Students attending and graduating from the Anaheim Union High School District (AUHSD) make the City of Anaheim a better place to live. Say what? Yes, of course the district produces students who are better prepared for complex life, but am I claiming that while students are currently learning, and after they graduate, they are actually improving society? Yes. And they have done this organically and explicitly over the past decade (since 2014) without any permission. Moreover, almost everyone, young students to elderly community members, can describe aspects of how it was done and what challenges they are facing. The fact that the transformation is complex and people can still explain why it works and can go even deeper proves that "lived complexity" is not beyond the human brain. If anything, the human brain relishes and thrives—cognitively, emotionally, socially, morally—on such action. It is why our team joined AUHSD in late 2021 to understand what it was doing and learn how to spread their ideas and do more.[1] It is an honor to write the foreword to this impressive story, which is coming into its own at the very time that society so desperately needs a way out of a downward spiral—one that has been gaining momentum these past fifty years.

The seven chapters in this book, together and in relation to each other, nail just about every problem that has plagued system change. They don't finish the job, but they set us on the right pathway to address the major systemic issues that maintained the status so very long—what scholars call the "old grammar of schooling" and its dogged presence in the face of all the assaults to overturn it. Brazer and Matsuda demonstrate that deep beneficial transformation is possible and even practical, as the district tackles each major force of systemic change and its relationships. It works because the district has motivated and engaged everyone—students, parents, teachers, principals, community, local businesses, and postsecondary institutions. It is comprehensive, systemic change and involves the entire system.

AUHSD's vision is a set of simple but powerful goals: "To create a better world through an Unlimited You." There are seven core values: (1) model the five Cs: collaboration, creativity, critical thinking, communication, and compassion; (2) education must work for all students and not the other way around; (3) an asset-based instructional approach nurtures everyone's potential; (4) move the needle toward equity and justice; (5) vision, mission, and core values are delivered through instruction; (6) work in systems not silos; and (7) public schools should enhance democracy through student voice and problem-solving.

The seven chapters describe big, interrelated forces in the Anaheim story. The first involves changing the basic narrative.

CHAPTER 1: CHANGING THE NARRATIVE. By changing the narrative—the very nature of learning—AUHSD is "integrating twenty-first-century skills (affective development), technical skills (cognitive development), and elevation of youth voice and purpose with meaningful support from external partnerships educates students for purposeful life." A Career Preparedness System Framework (CPSF) guides students to find clear purposes and the capacity to achieve them. The goal is for every student to graduate with purpose and particular career pathways established while in secondary school. Not every detail is fixed, but advanced skills and knowledge and a sense of purpose guide the way. There are 28,000 students in AUHSD, which has twenty schools; 74 percent of students are socioeconomically disadvantaged, 69.55 percent are Hispanic, 13 percent are Asian, and 8 percent are white. Notably, at AUHSD we see a new set of outcomes, not the traditional tests but traditional academic subjects linked to twenty-first-century skills and technical skills related to career pathways.

CHAPTER 2: GENERATING POSITIVE CHANGE WITH SYSTEMS THINKING. Within the general framework of new purpose and guided careers, students are empowered to discover their values and beliefs as they find their voice (the ability to articulate what matters to them). Matsuda and team use a framework that they call "three-level chess," constantly developing and cross-checking within and across schools, the district, and the community. Greater autonomy is granted at each level, but so is the expectation that people interact within and across the three levels (in our own work, we call this "connected autonomy"). Within this triple-level intra- and interlevel interaction, the vision is "communicated broadly and deeply." Special emphasis is placed on human relations and collaboration including "permeable boundaries." Creative tensions are recognized and seen as valuable for navigating "I-ness" and "We-ness" in individual and group work. Resistance and motivation to change are treated as potential sources of breakthrough. Instructional leadership is valued and developed as the central office supports schools. Capstone projects are a key integrator as *all students* capture and present student-generated portfolios that are age- and context-appropriate. District leaders join and support principals, teacher leaders, and professional learning teams working with students.

CHAPTER 3: ADDRESSING EVERY STUDENT'S STORY, FOSTERING AGENCY. In our own work, we feature "student as change-maker" and go even further to "student as value-adder." It is easy to think that you are going deep on this dimension without realizing that student agency and voice can be superficial. Students' presence must be deeply tied into the agenda of transforming culture and its deep practices. Individual depth is essential for students and families who have been mired in disadvantage. In Anaheim, for example, there are 1,650 homeless children. "Elevating student voice and purpose" constitutes understanding students and their families on multiple dimensions. In Anaheim, most families struggle with basic needs. The only way to have a chance on this dimension is to get to know every student by name and story. Context and individual circumstance are crucial. The CPSF is explicitly designed to address all the key interrelated needs: affective, cognitive, and dispositional according to life circumstances, including ethnicity. Students in Anaheim often attend various secondary schools, after moving households more than once. Classrooms as communities are tied to the notion that teachers learn about their students as individuals. Making classrooms psychologically and physically safe is key. A sense of community is fostered through routines of collaboration and compassion. There is a major emphasis on "scoping the world of work." CPSF is no ordinary guidance counseling service. It is designed to help each student graduate with a life plan and some capacity to pursue it.

CHAPTER 4: BUILDING A NETWORK TO ELEVATE YOUTH VOICE AND PURPOSE. Each of the essential elements of the CPSF is designed to overlap and reinforce the others. This is what is meant by systemic reinforcement. New technologies—AI, cybersecurity, biotechnology, and related partnerships and internships with advanced technology industries—enable students to get started early and develop skills, knowledge, and relationships with cutting-edge companies. Partnerships have been established with community colleges and civic organizations, resulting in a marked increase in dual-enrollment opportunities. Over 60 percent of students take one or more Career and Technical Education pathway courses. Another program, Anaheim Innovative Mentoring Experience (AIME), enables students to intern in local technology companies such as Loko.ai where students work on artificial intelligence. These experiences elevate student voice, while developing life purpose. Students are required to integrate their work in a culminating Capstone project. With guidance from a teacher mentor, students select their most meaningful work over the four years of high school "to present their portfolios and mastery of key skills—including the 5Cs—and knowledge they have acquired to a panel composed of several volunteers from the school community."

CHAPTER 5: MINDFULNESS AND THE FIFTH C. You don't swing from learning to well-being and back again. *You integrate them.* That's exactly what Brazer and Matsuda describe here: "As we claim throughout the book, integration of twenty-first-century skills with technical skills is a necessary condition for success in school, at work, at home, and in the community." Integration of the 5Cs and subject teaching is one route to balance and focus. Compassion, the fifth C, is essential for students and teachers engaged in educating for purposeful life.

CHAPTER 6: TEACHER PROFESSIONAL LEARNING. As with each of these big forces, leaders have to ensure that new professional learning is present and that it is integrated with all the other forces. The authors build in Elmore's claim—for every new skill area requirement, we need to provide commensurate capacity-building to acquire desired skills. To help improve teachers' skills and knowledge, curriculum specialists and (what I consider to be a brilliant move) 5Cs coaches work together to design and implement professional learning. As the authors say, "when curriculum specialists and 5Cs coaches engage in professional learning, the intended outcome is that 5Cs coaches take what they learn and work with teachers in their school sites." This ties in with CPSF work, particularly Capstone projects. Moreover, further integration occurs alongside the development of California's multibillion-dollar initiative for Community Schools (CSs). AUHSD weaves the new CS opportunities "into school life with explicit curriculum and pedagogy aligned with CPSF." The AUHSD initiative has provided new money to integrate community and school issues (such as health care, affordable housing, healthy-food availability). At the same time, there is a major expansion of Career and Technical Education (CTE) pathways, including several novel fields that have not yet become part of initial teacher education programs. CTE is greatly enhanced by AIME, which provides mentoring to open classrooms to the outside world to learn about new occupations that are just emerging.

CHAPTER 7: THE PROMISE OF THE CAREER PREPAREDNESS SYSTEMS FRAMEWORK. Chapter 7 is a reflection and reckoning with the reader that poses questions for the immediate future. In their "Food for Thought 7.1" prompt, Brazer and Matsuda ask:

> What sort of potential partners exist in your school district's community? Are there community colleges, retailers, ranchers, research facilities, manufacturing plants, social service agencies, farmers, nonprofits, and other service providers striving to strengthen your community? Are they committed to finding the next generation of innovators and leaders? In what ways does your student population align with philanthropic organizations committed to urban, suburban, or rural education?

We have had a big gulp of uncertainty in the past three years. The next period—2023–2025—promises even more. The authors give us a head start by offering a list of what matters: leadership, narrative, politics, voice, and patience. My message is "go deep with an interrelated set of forces." My message is don't underestimate what "deep" entails. AUHSD is not just a list of seven forces. The seven are deep in an interrelated way. They are organic, which means that they are beneath the surface, connected in ways not observable, in the soil that nurtures what is above and is cultivated or destroyed depending on what is happening above.

David Brazer, Mike Matsuda, and all the Anaheim educators have provided a wonderful example of what is possible and even insights for how to go about it.

Thank you for taking us to new terrain, so badly needed if we are to have any future. It alone is a thriving, creative one that refashions the future. What a magnificent accomplishment!

—Michael Fullan, OC, former dean; professor
emeritus, Faculty of Education, University of Toronto;
codirector, New Pedagogies for Deep Learning

INTRODUCTION

WRITING THIS BOOK has been a personal journey we have taken as partners. It reflects the past ten years of transformational work carried out by Superintendent Michael Matsuda, the dedicated educators of the Anaheim Union High School District, and committed community partners. Understanding our personal perspectives helps you, the reader, to make connections between experiences that have shaped us as educators and authors and the remarkable educational work we present in this book. We start with our points of view, then explain the purpose and structure of the book.

In 2017, on the seventy-fifth anniversary of Executive Order 9066, I (Michael) led a field trip to Manzanar, a national historic site. More than 110,00 Japanese Americans, most of whom were US citizens, were removed from their homes near the West Coast to remote, desert incarceration centers like Manzanar during World War II. Their ostensible crime was that they posed a danger to the United States. The internment left a deep scar on my Japanese parents, my family, and me. I hoped that our two busloads of students and teachers from the Anaheim Union High School District would understand the dangers and injustice of race-based policies and beliefs by confronting the inhumane conditions of Manzanar.

While on a tour of one of the barracks that showcased the squalid conditions—open toilets and rickety beds, with nothing but straw for mattresses—a student behind me said, "Wow, this is pretty nice." I turned around and asked him to explain what he meant. The student, a young Latino boy, looked me straight in the eye and said, "At least they had a place to sleep. I sleep with my brother on the garage floor." How far have we really come since Manzanar?

My thoughts turned to how this boy and I and countless other people of color are now integrated into society. A few generations ago, we lived in a segregated society, and we should be grateful. But to this day, his words haunt me, and I think about him, his future, and that of so many others. Discrimination and injustice are more subtle and more insidious than they were over seventy-five years ago. Is this boy's garage floor his Manzanar?

One of economics professor Raj Chetty's research claims speaks to the impact of economic inequality for youth who don't have a bed to sleep in and those who do:

> For white Americans, achieving the American Dream is like climbing a ladder... You pretty much start off where you left off in the previous generation and go up from there. For black Americans (and other marginalized groups) it's more like being on a treadmill. You rise up in one generation and there are tremendous structural forces that seem to push you back down in the income distribution, only to have to make the climb again.[1]

Despite educators' best intentions, too often and for too long, public schools have been one of the important structural forces that subordinate nonwhite, low-income, immigrant students and students with disabilities. Operating like factories that sort students based not on their inherent abilities or talents, but on how they answer fact-based questions on standardized tests, most schools do not provide the social and economic mobility our society summarizes as the American Dream. The factory model that has dominated secondary education from the dawn of the high school movement in the late nineteenth century to the present has shackled the latent creative and innovative energies of students, culminating in a lack of faith in the promise of what public schools purport to deliver.

In my nearly thirty years as a public school educator, I have been searching for ways to unshackle secondary students, to honor their personal stories and help them overcome obstacles that stand in their way. My opportunity as superintendent has been to build systems that move the Anaheim Union High School District away from the factory model and toward an institution that fulfills the promise of schools as opportunity engines. Make no mistake, this transformative model is not a "new shiny object." Placing teachers and instruction at the forefront of change requires stepwise, persistent, systemic commitment to a new North Star. The work is complicated, complex, and at times discouraging, but we have made substantial progress preparing young people for meaningful careers and life. In 2021, I invited David Brazer to join me in writing this book so that we could show the world what we have accomplished in Anaheim, how we have been able to change the meaning of secondary school education, where we have succeeded and the work that remains to be done, and how other districts might engage in educating for purposeful life.

I (David) came to know Michael Matsuda gradually through my role as the director of professional learning at TeachFX, a startup education technology company headed by one of my former students. As I learned more about the programs that supported the major education reform described in this book, I became a strong advocate for Michael's vision and the creative work of the remarkably gifted educators who work in the Anaheim Union High School District. I had not dreamed of writing a book such as this on the evening that Michael invited me to the project, but I had no hesitation when I agreed. As I told Michael at the time, he and his team were achieving what I had only vaguely dreamed of as a high school teacher and principal in the 1980s and 1990s. I am honored to help tell the story that addresses my passions for engaging teaching and learning and creative leadership. It gives me the opportunity to apply lessons learned from a career that started in the classroom and moved through school leadership, graduate teaching and research in education leadership, and a brief stint in education technology. For that, I am grateful.

Our collaboration in school reform in Anaheim and the process of writing this book has made us more than colleagues. We talk often as friends, blurring the lines between the professional and the personal. We have grown together through our work on behalf of students, parents, teachers, administrators, and the community and through telling this story. We hope that you will be as engaged in this book as we are in the work and that you will help us start a national dialogue about educating for purposeful life that will change the meaning of secondary school in the lives of current and future generations of students.

WHAT IS IN STORE

Our intent is that we have written a book that explains to educators, policy makers, parents, and interested members of communities across the United

States what it means to educate for purposeful life. We have framed what has been accomplished so far in Anaheim starting from posing a problem we have introduced here—schools as they have existed for a long time do not fulfill their promise as social mobility ladders. We follow with a discussion of the organizational framework we are employing to make positive change happen. From there, the story turns to understanding Anaheim's students, learning about programs that drive the reform, and how professional learning builds educators' capacities to educate students in different and promising ways. Throughout, we strive to reveal *how* programs and practices were developed, implemented, and refined so that readers can visualize how they might reorient secondary schools in their districts and communities.

CHAPTER 1. Readers are introduced to the Anaheim Union High School District and Superintendent Matsuda. We set the stage for the rest of the book by describing the district's recent history and the need for reform to build a brighter future for students and a stronger community within Anaheim and Orange County. The reform itself is embodied in the Career Preparedness Systems Framework (CPSF) that brings together initiatives past, present, and future into a coherent movement toward educating for purposeful life.

CHAPTER 2. To be able to adapt and apply initiatives from one district to another requires understanding how these initiatives were conceived, implemented, modified, and institutionalized. To aid in this process, we provide an organizational framework that will help other districts move their bureaucracies, educators, students, and parents toward profoundly changed classroom and out-of-school experiences. We employ systems thinking, human relations, organizational learning, and instructional leadership as anchor concepts that describe the systems work required to change a model of schooling that has endured for over a hundred years.

CHAPTER 3. We believe that knowing who the students in Anaheim are is a critical piece of the reader's perspective. We want readers to understand how the student populations in their districts are similar to and different from those educated by the Anaheim Union High School District. This chapter presents the demographics in easily digested form and discusses the implications for this population's learning. In brief, we explain the needs of a student population that is nearly 75 percent low-income, majority Latino, and homeless to a shocking degree.

CHAPTER 4. This chapter addresses the logical question readers will have in mind: What are you doing about the problems you have identified and how is it affecting this student population? We begin by demonstrating how the CPSF has helped district students succeed at a high level in terms of traditional measures that include standardized tests and college matriculation and persistence. We then spotlight three major initiatives within the CPSF: (1) connecting schools and the community through careers and work, (2) attending to students' affective needs in the classroom in a manner integrated with cognitive development, and (3) elevating student voice and purpose via meaningful learning experiences and reflection captured in portfolios and capstone experiences. These initiatives are illustrative, not comprehensive. We use our framework from chapter 2 to help readers understand what is going on systemically behind the scenes that produces outcomes that demonstrate substantial progress toward educating for purposeful life.

CHAPTER 5. Change is hard work and stressful. Adolescents are by definition changing every day, which puts them under stress. As their teachers are learning new ways to structure learning and new classroom practices, they will feel stress and anxiety too. For these reasons, we believe it is important to emphasize the district's focus on mindfulness. The practical step of an internal check-in when feeling an emotional reaction can help calm our inner and outer worlds. In Anaheim, this practice has been combined with one of the central instructional principles at work—compassion—to give added purpose to mindfulness. Treating students compassionately and helping them to be compassionate with one another, especially under stress, can happen more consistently when practicing mindfulness. Major reforms must have avenues for dealing with stress or they will die under the weight of it.

CHAPTER 6. We agree with Richard Elmore, who has said in several different ways that when we expect more from educators, leaders have an obligation to build their capacity to deliver more.[2] Chapter 6 describes three major approaches to professional learning employed by the Anaheim Union High School District. We keep professional learning within our organizational framework to demonstrate connections among structures, roles, and practices. The district's Community Schools program gives an opportunity to share one more innovative program while explaining its professional learning needs and how they are being addressed.

CHAPTER 7. The book concludes with reflection on how far we have come and the work ahead. We hope that our communication of lessons learned from striving to reform public education will guide educators who want to join with us to educate for purposeful life.

As you can no doubt see by now, we are proud of the changes happening in the Anaheim Union High School District and their effects on students' lives now and in the future. We recognize that the district is building on ideas established by others while creating novel approaches of its own. What is undoubtedly new and different is the way in which good ideas are being woven together, implemented, and improved. We hope you will agree and that reading this book will inspire you to make this kind of difference for young people where you live and work.

CHAPTER 1

CHANGING THE NARRATIVE

> The questions that we think face the country are questions which in one sense are much deeper than civil rights. They're questions which go very much to the bottom of mankind and people. They're questions which have repercussions in terms of . . . international affairs and relations. They're questions which go to the very root of our society. What kind of society will we be?
> —BOB MOSES, FOUNDER, ALGEBRA PROJECT,
> SPEECH ON FREEDOM SUMMER, 1964[1]

> The documented record . . . is mixed as to whether those reforms, including No Child Left Behind (NCLB), aimed at producing skilled graduates who could enter an information-driven workplace, achieved the intended goals. Since the early 2000s, high school graduation rates have risen. And, yes, the percentage of high school graduates attending college has increased. But test score gains sufficient to close the achievement gap between minorities and whites have not improved. Nor is there much evidence that graduates are better prepared to enter the workplace than an earlier generation. Furthermore, the promise that higher standards and accountability would alter historic inequalities between minorities and whites remains unfulfilled.
> —LARRY CUBAN, PROFESSOR EMERITUS, STANFORD UNIVERSITY, 2021[2]

THIS BOOK TELLS the inside story of the recent and ongoing effort by the Anaheim Union High School District (AUHSD) to address the yet unfulfilled promises identified by Moses and Cuban in the quotations that begin this chapter. We accept Cuban's criticisms of school reform movements of the past hundred years; they serve as red flags and cautionary tales for the efforts documented here.³ Our overarching thesis is that to reach students traditionally isolated from the best that school systems have to offer, and their more privileged peers, schools must meet students' learning needs in a comprehensive fashion that recognizes and affirms their individual life experiences. AUHSD takes the position that integrating twenty-first-century skills (affective development), technical skills (cognitive development), and elevation of youth voice and purpose with meaningful support from external partnerships educates students for purposeful life. Educating the whole student in this way requires reduced emphasis on federal testing mandates for English language arts and mathematics. The district does not "teach to the test." Neither state- nor district-generated interim assessments are used. AUHSD has shifted focus to creating a new system that weaves together classroom and community experiences in a deliberate, coordinated fashion that will substantially increase graduates' potential to achieve prosperous and gratifying adulthood while enriching the communities where they live. For school districts to foster equity, develop high-performing graduates, and enhance civic engagement in local communities, the education they provide must help adolescents learn who they are and how to engage with peers and adults as preparation for addressing society's greatest challenges.

More than a century of challenges embedded in the bureaucracies we call school districts remain, requiring innovative approaches for organizing, leading, teaching, and learning. What that means specifically is explained in later chapters. First, we briefly discuss fundamental current trends and give an overview about what AUHSD is doing to address them in grades 7–12.

THE CHANGING WORLDS OF SECONDARY EDUCATION AND WORK

Since the passage of the GI Bill in 1944, generations of Americans have had unprecedented access to higher education, which arguably fueled the country's development into the world's greatest economic superpower for over seventy-five years. With rapid growth in demand for higher education, California and other states adopted education master plans in the 1960s to provide cohesion across college and university hierarchies. In California, this meant clarifying the missions of community colleges, the California State University system, and the University of California system. From the 1960s on, higher education systems across the country created more access for minorities and women. Since the end of World War II, the mantra for young Americans has been that going to college and getting a degree is the path to economic and social mobility and a bright future. The promotion of this fundamental belief has intensified in the first two decades of the twenty-first century for many reasons.

At the beginning of the post–World War II surge in higher education, public university was relatively cheap, well-paying jobs were plentiful, and health insurance had become a common benefit of full-time employment. These features of the US economy were easily accessed by white middle-class households. But the economic shifts of the 1980s mark a watershed as tuition rose much faster than the cost of living—169 percent in that decade—while income for young workers rose by just 19 percent.[4]

The report that compares higher education cost increases with income for those new in the workforce also indicts the United States' fragmented system of education and workforce development:

> The evidence of our failure to help all youth make the long journey from early childhood to adult economic independence is plain. In the trajectory from kindergarten to a good job, the most talented disadvantaged youth do not fare nearly as well as the least talented advantaged youth . . . It is far better to be born rich and white than smart and poor in America.[5]

Moreover, according to an Oxford University study, technology is likely to eliminate almost half of all jobs in the next few decades.[6] In addition, the employability gap—the gap between what skills employers need and what skills workers have—is growing larger. Our school systems are failing to address the skills development challenge adequately.[7] Occupations in the skilled trades, information technology, sales and marketing, driving and logistics, construction, customer support, and health care are some of the most prominent jobs employers are having trouble filling in the United States.

Economic, social, and political changes over the decades from the 1960s to the 2020s have greatly influenced students' educational experiences, particularly for lower-income households with children of color or children with special needs. The proportion of households in poverty or on the margin has grown as the wealth gap has widened and community support of public education has eroded.[8] To provide a glimpse of how these changes have impacted high school graduates and the promise of a brighter future, we present two brief vignettes—one from Brazer's experience as a high school principal in the 1990s and one from Matsuda's contemporary experience as AUHSD superintendent.

1990S HIGH SCHOOL GRADUATE

Anjelica started out high school in an advanced level of what was then called English as a Second Language. With low grades coming out of middle school, she started ninth grade in pre-algebra, non-laboratory science for English language learners, standard ninth-grade English, and a world studies course. Anjelica was a compliant student who earned mostly Cs and Ds, with some Bs and a few As. She followed her postgraduation plan and attended the local community college, not really considering four-year college and not interested in moving away from home. Anjelica was frustrated in community college by the need to take remedial math and English to be able to move on to four-year college courses. Her dream of completing community college with a certificate or degree gradually faded behind a rationale that she needed to work to contribute to family income. After two years of sporadic course taking, Anjelica stopped attending community college in favor of working full-time at Costco.

TODAY'S HIGH SCHOOL GRADUATE

Anthony also started high school as an English language learner. Like many of his peers, Anthony was not thinking about his future. His mind was focused on just staying out of trouble. But one day Anthony was handed a flier in school that offered a chance to take a college class while still a senior, a class that would teach him how to "hack the internet." Through a district partnership with a local community college, Anthony concurrently enrolled in cybersecurity courses. Anthony might have been vulnerable to opting for a low-paying job after graduation, such as following in his father's footsteps as a day laborer, but he was able to use what he learned about network security to land an entry-level job at Hulu that pays $65,000. Anthony secured this job upon high school graduation and continues to work full-time while he attends community college. Today, he articulates the significance of his first professional job and expresses civic engagement values he learned in high school when he says, "It's a field that I love and find meaning [in] because I know I am making a difference protecting ordinary people from being hacked as well as contributing to my company's bottom line." Anthony's sense of purpose is so strong that he now mentors a student from his former high school and encourages him and others to enter cybersecurity work.

Anjelica and Anthony began high school in similar places in their different decades, but Anthony developed a direction and sense of purpose Anjelica was not able to find in her first few postgraduate years. Both had access to dual enrollment at local community colleges, but only Anthony took advantage of the opportunity. Two important distinctions helped create a different outcome for Anthony: (1) the dual-enrollment courses he took led directly into a career, and (2) his high school fostered his development as an inspired adult while teaching him a curriculum that helped him to thrive in a work setting he found attractive. Anthony's advantage derived from a changed vision of what it means to attend and graduate from high school in AUHSD.

Graduating with Purpose

The 1990s narrative represents Brazer's years as a high school principal in the San Francisco Bay Area. Frustrated by the "pretend college preparation" scenario of students moving through high school, graduating ineligible to apply to four-year colleges because of poor grades in college preparatory courses, and unable to succeed in community college, he tried to work with local community colleges to create meaningful transitions for students. Gatekeepers such as advanced algebra and laboratory science generated great frustration for students such as Anjelica. Brazer's attempts to create new pathways in culinary arts and automotive technology saw limited success in opening doors for students not well served by the standard college preparatory curriculum. Although still in place more than twenty-five years later, these programs serve a small number of students who may matriculate into community college and advance into careers that have meaning for them. Typical of most high schools today, Brazer's school had no community-based support network for students as they matured and pursued life after high school.

Anthony's experience is the fruit of Superintendent Matsuda's push to change the high school narrative in AUHSD. Instead of Brazer acting as a lone principal cobbling together small programs dependent on the availability and expertise of unusual teachers, Matsuda has taken a systemic approach that captures the entire educational experience of secondary students. AUHSD is a changed system that educates all students differently compared to the 1990s or even just a few years ago. Anjelica had a vague notion that she wanted to move on with her education so she could get a good job. Anthony, in sharp contrast, graduated with a sense of purpose: "making a difference protecting ordinary people." Barely into the field of cybersecurity himself, he aspires to bring others along. This is the changing narrative: moving the district from test-based goals to life-based aspirations by graduating from high school with a sense of purpose; an understanding of the path to achieving that purpose; and the motivation, skills, and knowledge to achieve personal aspirations.

> *Food for Thought 1.1*
> What are the immediate prospects for high school graduates in your school or district? Do they have a viable, prosperous post–high school path? What are the most important indicators one way or the other?

The changing narrative in AUHSD is more complicated and more complex than the status quo experience for most students in public secondary education in the United States. Complication comes from the fact that schools meaningfully interacting with their communities generates many more moving parts. Curricula and pedagogy in AUHSD are changing to meet students' affective and cognitive development needs defined in large part by immigrant status and low family income. Beyond changing what happens inside schools, secondary education in AUHSD is no longer contained within the walls of its schools or the district as a whole. Numerous partners from various sectors of education and the economy are essential to the experiences of students like Anthony who are hired into high-paying jobs right out of high school, and even the students who head straight to four-year universities. Changing the menu of courses, using new teaching methods, and offering learning experiences grounded in the community bring far more complexity to the educational enterprise. Nevertheless, the complicated and complex attributes of changed education better position the school district to take advantage of community resources and opportunities on students' behalf. AUHSD's aspiration that students will graduate with advanced skills and knowledge and a sense of purpose requires agility to meet a wide range of student needs, develop teachers' capacity to teach in new ways, and keep community and educational partners engaged.

LIFE IN AUHSD

AUHSD, located in the shadow of Disneyland, serves over 28,000 students (2021–2022 enrollment) from five different communities in central Orange County, California. More than 1,200 teachers work in the district's schools. High school districts are not common across all fifty states, and AUHSD has a few characteristics that may seem quirky even among high school districts. As the name suggests, the district educates only secondary students, but not just high school students. Eight of the district's twenty comprehensive schools are junior high schools. A holdover term from before the middle school movement that began in the 1960s, these junior high schools enroll seventh and eighth graders who then move on to the district's ten comprehensive high schools or one of the specialty programs.

AUHSD's students are demographically diverse by most standards. In the 2021–2022 school year, over 74 percent of students were classified by the State of California as socioeconomically disadvantaged, more than 23 percent of the district's students were English language learners, and the largest racial group by far was Hispanic at 69.5 percent, followed by 13 percent Asian, and 8 percent white. Typical of most school districts, approximately 14 percent of AUHSD's student population were students with disabilities that year. Nearly 91 percent of the class of 2021 graduated from high school.[9]

The Superintendent

Superintendent Matsuda grew up in Orange County and has worked his entire career in education in AUHSD. The son of Japanese American parents who were sent to internment camps in World War II, Matsuda became the first person of color to serve as superintendent in 2014. His perspective:

> *For me, it's personal. On December 7, 1941—the day Japan bombed Peral Harbor—my mother was a freshman at Anaheim High School. A few months later, in an overt act of racial hostility, President Franklin Roosevelt signed Executive Order 9066, authorizing the internment of 120,000 individuals—most of whom were American citizens of Japanese descent. My mother, her five sisters, and her recently widowed father were among those imprisoned.*

> *I grew up in Orange County in the 1970s during the Vietnam War. Once again, the enemy was people of Asian descent. I have painful memories of being tormented by other kids who yelled racial slurs such as "chink" and "gook" at me. Forty years later, I became superintendent in AUHSD. Only in America.*
>
> *As positive as my own story turns out to be, for too many of our Generation Z students now in our school systems, ideals such as equal opportunity, social mobility, and the American Dream ring hollow. Instead of cultivating critical thinkers who are informed, engaged, and compassionate citizens with high potential to live prosperously in their community, we have cultivated a generation of test-takers and passive learners who do not trust each other, have little passion for education, and are increasingly disaffected and discouraged.*[10]

Matsuda's unusual path to superintendent did not include experience as an assistant principal or principal. Nevertheless, he has achieved national influence and been recognized as a "Leader to Learn from in 2016" (one of twelve nationally) by *EdWeek Magazine*; a "Visionary Leader" by California State University, Fullerton; for the California State "Champion of Civic Engagement Award"; for the University of California, Irvine, School of Education "Outstanding Community Partner Award"; and was recognized with an honorary doctorate from Chapman University for his dedication to youth and community.

Before becoming an educator in 1994, Matsuda was a contract negotiator for the Jet Propulsion Laboratory. In the late 1980s, he became an entrepreneur, involved in retail clothing and importing. However, by 1992, his entrepreneurship hit a dead end; he was broke and living with his parents. At this low point in his early adult life, Matsuda discovered a calling to teach while substituting in K–12 schools. Reading Viktor Frankl's *Man's Search for Meaning* helped Matsuda explain the sense of fulfillment and self-transcendence he discovered by making a difference in young people's lives. This life transition from business to education sparked Matsuda's belief that purposeful work, no matter the calling, was the key to a joyful and fulfilled life.

First hired as an English teacher at an AUHSD junior high school in 1994, Matsuda later taught ninth-grade English at Oxford Academy, an AUHSD magnet school. By 2000, he was working in the district office as a teacher on special assignment, helping to coordinate the teacher induction program. During this same period, Matsuda was appointed to an open seat on the North Orange County Community College District board of trustees in 2006. He successfully defended his seat in two subsequent elections. More than eight years working inside the school district and debating policy and operations for the local community college system taught Matsuda about regional politics, community members across the power spectrum, union issues, and the challenges of managing a large institution. By 2007, Matsuda's administrative responsibilities within the school district had expanded to include leading professional development and overseeing grants, including GEAR UP, the largest federal program serving minority and first-generation college-going students.[11]

Matsuda's perspective on civic engagement was expanded in 2012, two years before being named superintendent. Riots broke out in the streets of Anaheim in response to successive police killings of alleged gang members who were unarmed. The following year, Matsuda, along with a handful of teachers concerned about increasing tensions between law enforcement and students, helped organize students to convey their aspiration for better relationships between the city and schools. Anaheim mayor Tom Tait, having run on a platform that included kindness as a core value, encouraged the students to create a petition. In the fall of 2013, two hundred students delivered over five thousand signatures to the city council asking for internships and mentoring, along with a commitment to twenty-first-century education. This spontaneous interaction between students and their community inspired Matsuda to work toward affective development, student voice, and civic engagement. These are the centerpieces of his superintendency and the educational experience in AUHSD today.[12]

> *Food for Thought 1.2*
> How would you describe the relationships between your school district and the community(ies) it serves? What are some steps you might take to broaden and deepen these relationships?

VISION, MISSION, AND CORE VALUES

The AUHSD vision that guides work throughout the district is a simple statement imbued with ambition: "To create a better world through Unlimited

You."[13] The vision evolved over several years as elements of the district's major reform, titled Career Preparedness Systems Framework, began to take shape. As the district was changing course, AUHSD worked with a marketing firm to craft a message that would speak to parents, teachers, students, and the community.[14]

The AUHSD mission statement specifies what is meant by the concepts in the vision. It too has evolved over time as district personnel have worked to articulate a mission that reorients the district and the community from a test-based focus to educating competent, motivated, and empowered young adults:

> The Anaheim Union High School District, in partnership with the greater community, will graduate socially aware, civic-minded students who are life ready by cultivating the hard and soft skills.[15]

The vision and mission that drive decision-making and action in AUHSD have implied ideals, made explicit by the district's published core values. The core values listed below serve as a set of standards by which educators are able to assess their decisions and actions.

We believe . . .

1. *In and model the 5Cs*: Collaboration, Creativity, Critical Thinking, Communication and Compassion
2. That education *must work for students* and not the other way around
3. In an *assets-based* instructional *approach* focused on our community's strengths and in nurturing everyone's potential
4. In moving the needle toward *equity and justice*
5. That our vision, mission, and core values are delivered primarily through *instruction*
6. In *systems* not silos
7. Public schools should enhance and strengthen democracy through *cultivation of student voice and problem solving*.[16]

Vision, mission, and core values are taken seriously in AUHSD. They are a part of the discourse among school leaders and teachers, and Matsuda and his central office leadership team strive to keep them that way. One essential technique Matsuda uses is to develop school leaders into systems thinkers based on Senge's *The Fifth Discipline*, Kofman's *Conscious Business*, and other sources.[17] Specifically, he encourages school and district leaders to consider their current education aspirations and achievements relative to the district's vision. Senge refers to this kind of thinking as identifying the opportunity or space for creative tension (see figure 1.1).[18] Matsuda pushes central office and school site leaders to use creative tension to achieve reform goals within their spheres of influence and leadership responsibilities, clearly understanding that the district vision comes first.

Kofman helps us to think about how people approach creative tension through three different perspectives. He refers to a schema that includes "It, We, and I." "It" is the district purpose as articulated in the vision, mission, and core values. "We" is how educators within AUHSD collectively align their work to refocus and improve instruction with the vision. "I" refers to how individuals see their role and purpose to help students "create a better world through Unlimited You," whether that is in the classroom, as a principal, or working in one of the divisions of the district office. Each of these relationships requires work and self-awareness to stay aligned with the district vision while managing individual and group relationships. Kofman's It, We, and I provide a simple device for knowing the system's purpose and one's role, both individually and collectively, in it.[19] Figure 1.2 provides examples using typical school district roles.

Our discussion of AUHSD's vision, mission, and core values is intended to reveal the driving concepts behind the district's long-term effort to move secondary education from test based to life based. Each district must formulate its own vision, mission, and core values that are appropriate for its aspirations

FIGURE 1.1 *Creative tension derived from the difference between current reality and the district vision*

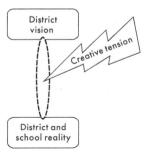

FIGURE 1.2 *How "I" and "We" address the "It" of the district vision*

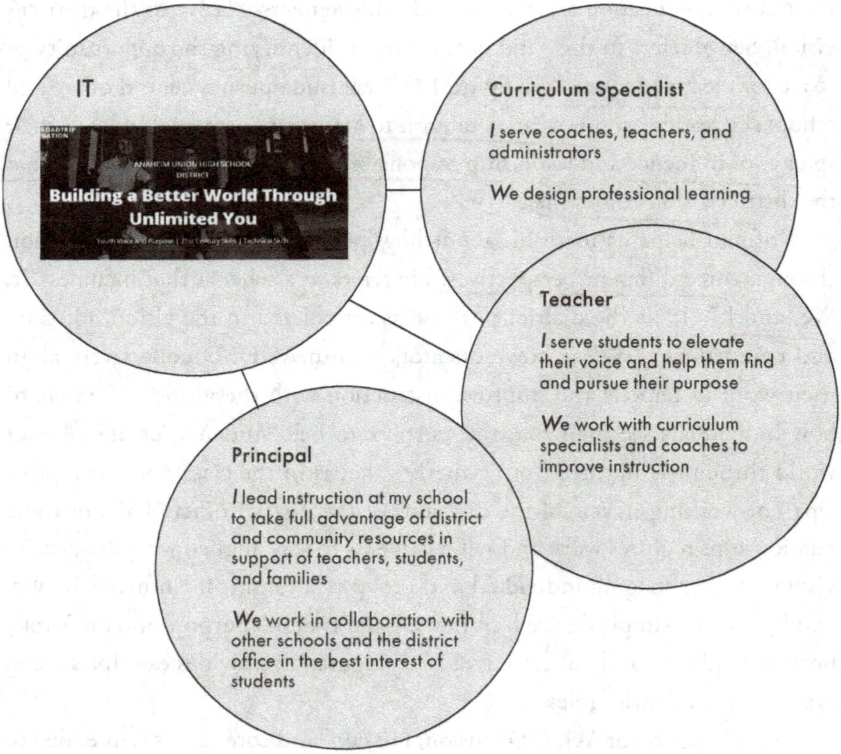

IT
Building a Better World Through Unlimited You
ANAHEIM UNION HIGH SCHOOL DISTRICT
Youth Voice and Purpose | 21st Century Skills | Technical Skills

Curriculum Specialist
I serve coaches, teachers, and administrators

We design professional learning

Teacher
I serve students to elevate their voice and help them find and pursue their purpose

We work with curriculum specialists and coaches to improve instruction

Principal
I lead instruction at my school to take full advantage of district and community resources in support of teachers, students, and families

We work in collaboration with other schools and the district office in the best interest of students

and context. Knowing what they are in AUHSD helps illustrate for education professionals and researchers the theories of action employed to make meaningful change for students.[20] The details of and rationale for the change are embedded in AUHSD's Career Preparedness Systems Framework, built on the vision, mission, and core values.[21]

THE PATHWAY TOWARD EMPOWERED HIGH SCHOOL GRADUATES: THE CPSF

The Career Preparedness Systems Framework (CPSF) articulates a new narrative for what it means to be a high school graduate who possesses a clear sense of purpose and the capacity to achieve it. In this chapter, we focus on what the CPSF means for students. Chapter 2 explains how the district is organized to make the systems in the framework coherent and mutually reinforcing.

The following section describes the context, rationale, and general descriptors embedded in the CPSF to convey the aspirations of this new approach to secondary education.[22] Figure 1.3 is the district's CPSF graphic, comprising three essential drivers: youth voice and purpose, twenty-first-century skills, and technical skills.[23]

Twenty-First-Century Skills: Affective Development

Early in Matsuda's tenure as superintendent, he promoted classroom-based affective supports for students' cognitive growth. This was imperative because of the high poverty rate of the district's student population and the social and psychological challenges that low-income immigrant status brings to youth in secondary schools. Matsuda credits much of the transition instructionally to the P21 Partnership, a national coalition of forward-thinking corporations, nonprofits, and public school institutions based in Washington, DC, that conceptualized affective development as foundational for career and college readiness. Matsuda broadened the P21 student characteristics to include compassion in response to the growing need for belongingness, mental health awareness, and character development. Operationalizing P21, teachers were encouraged to incorporate the 5Cs—a set of dispositions that would help students to develop into young, caring adults—into their teaching. AUHSD's version of the 5Cs had its origins in a somewhat different form in one of the district's high schools. Today, they are captured in the words and phrases:

FIGURE 1.3 *Career Preparedness Systems Framework (CPSF)*

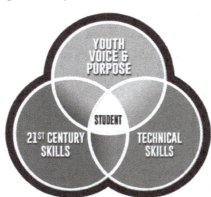

(1) Communication, (2) Collaboration, (3) Critical Thinking, (4) Creativity, and (5) Compassion. AUHSD's 5Cs are elaborated in a document available to all district staff, including rubrics for student development that use the descriptors "emerging, progressing, excelling."[24]

The 5Cs taken together describe a student who thinks and communicates effectively in multiple modes while developing the characteristics of being a valued member of a community inside the classroom and in the wider world. They are not just an add-on, something to be addressed in an advisory period, for example. Rather, they are intended to be woven into daily teaching and learning. They serve one of AUHSD's valued student outcomes that we will reference often: elevated voice and purpose.[25]

Returning to vision, mission, and core values, the 5Cs are prominently embedded implicitly and explicitly. The mission emphasizes twenty-first-century skill development, operationalized through the 5Cs, with the phrases "socially aware" and "civic-minded" in reference to graduates. Similarly, explicit reference to hard and soft skills communicates the need for cognitive and affective development to work interdependently in classrooms. The purpose of integrating hard and soft skills also comes from the mission in the phrase "life ready," which means that students are prepared for career options and civic and social responsibility. The 5Cs are further reinforced through explicit mention in the core values.

Acting on the core values in a manner that pursues the larger vision and mission is a subtle process. Acknowledging that operationalization may need to be different for different schools, AUHSD provides a large measure of autonomy to address the district's learning objectives in a manner consistent with the vision, mission, and goals. The system encourages innovation and tolerates variation to pursue the vision. As an example, before Matsuda became superintendent, Savanna High School developed a precursor to the 5Cs and instituted a culminating experience for graduating seniors called the Capstone project.[26] Students gather a portfolio of their work and development over their four years in high school and engage in a panel interview process in the spring of their senior year. In that interview, they are expected to explain their 5Cs development, supported by evidence from their portfolio. This reflection on a student's high school career and the metacognition that results are intended to demonstrate to students and members of the public how they have grown in terms of communication and character development while demonstrating their abilities in the interview process. The Capstone project as structured in AUHSD results from instruction, consistent with the fifth core value that "[t]he vision, mission, and core values are delivered primarily through instruction."

As an interview panel member for Savanna High School, Brazer has paid particular attention to students' sense of purpose upon graduation. Students' development naturally varies, but Capstone interviews demonstrate that teachers and students have emphasized the 5Cs during these students' secondary school careers such that when students graduate, they have grown and developed affectively as well as cognitively. One vivid example comes from a student who explained that he was diagnosed with autism in seventh grade. Upon entering high school, he set the goal of becoming more socially engaged. As a graduating senior, he explained to the panel the deliberate steps he took to achieve his goal, providing specific evidence of his efforts and their positive results.

Technical Skills: Cognitive Development

Twenty-first-century skills development enhances and does not supplant cognitive development and academic achievement. AUHSD's schools are striving to teach students the academic subjects they need in order to succeed in postsecondary education and beyond—just like schools across the nation. And the district works to narrow learning gaps for the special populations that comprise a majority of the student body—low-income, special education, and English language learner students. Beyond subjects addressed in the Common Core State Standards adopted by California and electives attractive to adolescents such as visual and performing arts, AUHSD is reimagining career and technical education (CTE) in two ways. The first is discovering and participating in CTE courses that inspire students to enter the world of work. This goal is for all students, not just those who may not imagine themselves attending four-year university, to use the pathways for discovery. Second, a "career" needs to be durable for the next twenty to thirty years in order for students to have promising futures. This latter point means that students' learning experiences cannot be anchored in the jobs they might attain in the short term. Instead, their pathway must lead them to an uncertain destination for which near-term jobs are just a starting point. The 5Cs integrated with technical skills development give students the capacity to navigate an uncertain job market.

Getting students to explore the realities of career pathways helps them develop a sense of purpose before graduating, just like Anthony's experience with cybersecurity. Illustrative examples of new, career-oriented curricula in AUHSD, developed in partnership with local companies, nonprofit organizations, and higher education, include programs in artificial intelligence, biotechnology, entrepreneurship, agriscience, and four programs certified by Google. Technical skills required by these and other pathways build on and vary from those found in the core curricula of English language arts, mathematics, social studies, and science. Many of the CTE pathways offered in AUHSD are in cutting-edge areas that have been identified by regional and national business partners as vital to economic growth, especially in low-income communities where so many students are ill-prepared for much needed STEAM careers.[27] Emphasizing CTE across a broad spectrum and for all students opens doors to the world beyond high school boundaries.

Learning Beyond the High School Campus

Twenty-first-century skills and technical skills are integrated when applied in partnership with higher education (both community college and four-year universities). Community college partnerships are anchored in the district's dual-enrollment program. As the name implies, high school and college credits are earned simultaneously from a single course, helping students build a transcript that accelerates their time to a certificate, associate's degree, or bachelor's degree. College credit is intended to be aligned with a student's career pathway and is offered at the high school site either during or after school. When community college partners send instructors to school sites, dual enrollment expands course offerings that traditional high schools often find difficult to provide because teachers lack credentials in emerging workforce pathways. Biotechnology, cybersecurity, and artificial intelligence are just a few examples where community college faculty are meeting dual-enrollment needs.

External nonprofit and business partners provide vital links to the world of work emphasized in AUHSD's approach to education encompassed by the CSPF. Mentorships and internships provide essential learning experiences and connections between students and future employers. To date, AUHSD has engaged over ninety-five partners from for-profit and nonprofit enterprises, offering myriad opportunities for adult mentoring from AI to aerospace to health care to culinary arts and hospitality. After a careful matching process that connects student interests with internship opportunities, students work for a semester or more to fulfill responsibilities defined by the internship site. For example, Brazer and the company he worked for prior to this writing routinely hosted interns in the areas of sales, product, and professional learning. Students completed their internships with specific work products they could feature as part of their Capstone experience.

Student Voice and Purpose

Students find their voices in classroom learning experiences when asked to express themselves about issues that matter to them, take action motivated by their point of view, and reflect on results. With multiple avenues for self-discovery (discussed in later chapters), students have opportunities to gauge how their thinking and self-concept have changed when they engage in culminating experiences such as the Capstone showcase. Classroom experiences give students the strength and confidence to engage in their communities.

Civic engagement is about community-building beyond contributing to the local economy. Students may become involved in their community spontaneously (as in the 2012 example), complete a class assignment or project, or participate in a civically engaged internship. Students are encouraged to address issues of importance to them, which may range from providing healthy food to impoverished communities (a project spawned by the agriscience program) to working on issues such as homelessness, mental health, and climate change. Civic engagement is generally based in the community where the school district is located to make the closest connection to students' lived experiences and to demonstrate that their voice and actions make a difference.

Students discover their voices when they are given opportunities to speak up and discover how they might contribute to the worlds of work and society. Their purpose emerges in a structure that includes traditional classrooms, presentations from professionals, mentoring, and internships. Graduating with purpose requires a willingness to give students the time, space, and structure to learn about themselves and their aspirations. The combination of twenty-first-century skills and technical skills equips students to be aware of their own aspirations, identify life goals, and pursue those goals in higher education and a fulfilling career.

A NEW SET OF OUTCOMES

AUHSD graduates understand themselves as much more than a set of test scores with a diploma. They have taken the opportunity to begin defining who they wish to be as an adult member of the broader Anaheim and Orange County communities by learning traditional curricula, CTE curricula, civic engagement, and specialty areas such as innovation and entrepreneurship. The district's intentional development of students' skills, knowledge, and dispositions empowers graduates to pursue their life purpose into careers and higher education. Twenty-first-century skills and technical skills are mutually reinforcing and necessary conditions for developing youth voice and purpose. Proficiency in technical skills without twenty-first-century skills may lead to a "smart" graduate unable to work effectively with others or communicate insights. Twenty-first-century skills without technical skills may result in a socially adept graduate unable to find gratifying work in the local economy. Students strong in both who have discovered their voice and calling are far more likely to graduate into a purposeful life.

This overview of AUHSD and its signature reform—the CPSF—should generate many questions in readers' minds regarding program specifics and how they are being achieved. Answering these questions is the mission behind the remainder of this book. Our next step is to organize AUHSD's implementation of the CPSF into a structure with four main components: (1) systems thinking, (2) human relations, (3) organizational learning, and (4) instructional leadership. This discussion in chapter 2 generates a model for shifting the focus of education from testing and college preparation to preparing students for purposeful life. We use the concepts from chapter 2 to help us name and explain the actions and results featured in chapters 3–7.

> **TAKING STOCK: CHANGING THE NARRATIVE IN YOUR SCHOOL DISTRICT**
>
> We believe that one of the great values of reading this book is that it will stimulate your thinking about what is possible and needed in your own setting. To help you reflect, we provide an essential question or two along with a "Taking Stock" reflection at the end of each chapter.
>
> **Essential Questions**
>
> 1. Do most of your school district's graduates have a clear idea about work they will find fulfilling? Do they know how to go from high school to that work?
> 2. Are students learning twenty-first-century skills? In what ways? How do you know?
> 3. What opportunities are available in your district for students to connect with the local community and economy?
>
> You can use the checklist in table 1.1 to stimulate your thinking and generate reflections.
>
> **Reflections and Next Steps:**

TABLE 1.1 *Opportunities available to students*

	Not yet	Developing	Meaningful
Twenty-first-century skills valued in the community and workplace			
Technical skills needed in twenty-first-century higher education and work settings			
Connections among schools, district, and community			

CHAPTER 2

GENERATING POSITIVE CHANGE WITH SYSTEMS THINKING

> The more efficient you are at doing the wrong thing, the wronger you become. It is much better to do the right thing wronger than the wrong thing righter. If you do the right thing wrong and correct it, you get better.
>
> —RUSSELL L. ACKOFF[1]

GENERATING THE KIND of change envisioned in the CPSF requires well-functioning, coherent systems that guide the district's work through inevitable external shocks and influences. A recent shock—possibly the largest we will see for a long time—was the COVID-19 pandemic. It is a force that flattened civilization—stopped cars, factories, supply chains, schools, and normal day-to-day existence. It killed millions of people without discrimination and stifled in-person human discourse for nearly two years. The pandemic forced many school leaders into early retirement, leaving many survivors who seem to cling to a mental model of education based on what they knew before COVID-19. Matsuda and his team were on the move pre-pandemic, transforming AUHSD in a systemic, coherent manner. This external shock became the obstacle that showed the way forward. "The obstacle is the way."[2] There was no going back because AUHSD was focused on educating for purposeful life, no matter the local, temporary pressures.

To understand just how far forward the district had moved, nine representatives of central office departments and four "friends of AUHSD" who consult with the district gathered in a hotel conference room in Portland, Oregon, in mid-winter 2022. In-person schooling had resumed at the beginning of the academic year, but lingering pandemic effects were still felt. The group of over a dozen educators analyzed some of the district's systems in an effort to figure out next steps toward implementation of the CPSF. They recentered on AUHSD's vision, explored the district's organizational culture, identified bureaucratic levers and roadblocks, and planned specific implementation actions that would propel the CPSF forward. The weekend workshop was a reflective pause, a deliberate effort to understand and work within the multiple systems that comprise AUHSD. Everyone reaffirmed that implementing reform is more of a process than an event that requires taking advantage of opportunities and overcoming inertia.

Achieving systems coordination and coherence from the classroom through the district office and into the community is an enormous challenge. Much good work was happening in AUHSD for the benefit of students, but after more than eight years of changing the district's direction and numerous personnel changes, Matsuda felt the need to refocus district office leaders on the processes and responsibilities essential to bringing the CPSF to fruition.

This chapter explains the organizational framework AUHSD employs for making positive change within the nested organizations we call school districts. AUHSD applies systems thinking, human relations, organizational learning, and instructional leadership in practical ways to bring the CPSF to life and ensure its growth and development over time. By explaining a framework with these four major components, we provide a perspective from which readers can understand changes occurring in AUHSD and through which they can figure out positive change in their own schools, districts, and communities. This chapter presents the ideal case—what is intended—while subsequent chapters discuss the realities of success achieved and work yet to be done.

As we present a framework for initiating and managing reform, we do not wish to lose sight of the purpose for positive change described in this and subsequent chapters. Change in AUHSD, like all meaningful educational change, is motivated by and grounded in an elevating vision and mission—to enhance rather than squelch adolescents' self-discovery. Since 2014, Matsuda and his team have gradually shifted AUHSD toward empowering students to discover their values and beliefs as they find their voice (the ability to articulate what matters to them) while imagining a gratifying place in their community as they emerge into adulthood. The challenge at the conference in Portland was to figure out the next steps needed to sustain forward motion toward the district's vision, its North Star. The fundamental shift the district strives for is away from the sorting function schools have performed for over a hundred years and toward becoming engines of opportunity for students. In practical terms, this means creating access to fulfilling jobs and careers for students and cultivating aspirations to improve the community in which they live. The twin values of meaningful work and civic engagement derive from the Civil Rights Movement led by Martin Luther King Jr., Cesar Chavez, Bob Moses, Gloria Steinem, and many others. Thus, by being equity-driven, the CPSF guides the district office, school site leadership, and classroom teachers toward creating experiences that value and elevate student voice and the discovery of life purpose.

We wish to emphasize that educating for purposeful life is a process that embraces and expands on familiar coursework (e.g., core subject areas, world languages, and the arts) and employs standard achievement measures. But much more goes into educating for purposeful life. Students' affective and cognitive needs are seen as *intertwined*, rather than separate. Affective development provides motivation and inspiration. The result is time, attention, and resources being reallocated toward educating the whole student without compromising academic excellence. Knowing how to continue and expand this work requires a practical understanding of the structures, principles, and actions that generate positive change.

SYSTEMS THINKING—A GAME OF THREE-LEVEL CHESS

Senge's signature book, *The Fifth Discipline*, is intended to help readers see organizations in whole and in their various parts *simultaneously* to understand not just one or two operations, but to comprehend the interconnected nature of systems (consistent with theory and research, we use the terms *organization* and *system* interchangeably) within and around a particular organization. Moreover, Senge espouses the intentional development of systems as "learning organizations." Elaborating on learning organizations, Ackoff contends that social systems, as distinct from mechanical and individual actor systems, are capable of learning at the organizational level. The challenge, from Ackoff's point of view, is perceiving and understanding the social dynamics of structurally and human relations–based behaviors and actions.[3]

Matsuda and his team strive for a culture of learning happening at every level, from district cabinet and central office to site administrative teams, departments, and school leadership teams to teachers and students in classrooms. Explaining implementation of the CPSF, we specify schools, districts, higher education institutions, and for-profit and nonprofit entities as our systems of interest.[4] Each one of these entities is best understood as a social system and therefore amenable to learning. The district has multiple nested systems— the schools and systems within them—while systems from outside district boundaries, such as nonprofit institutions and community colleges, act interdependently with the school district and sometimes directly with schools. We emphasize the interconnected nature of all these systems to capture Senge's point that leaders striving to create learning organizations that improve need to understand how systems affect one another while accounting for their discrete parts and aggregate operations.

To simplify, we classify three essential systems this way: (1) schools, (2) the district, and (3) the community. Each of these systems is open, with permeable boundaries—that is, each is affected by and in turn affects another system. Beyond the community is the broader environment that has influence on all three systems but is of less interest to us for explaining the dynamics of the CPSF. Figure 2.1 is the first version of a diagram we will build throughout the chapter. It displays our main systems of interest and how they are positioned relative to one another. We use three-level chess as a metaphor to help us think about the simultaneity of these systems' processes and outcomes.

Three-level chess was popularized in the 1960s hit television series *Star Trek*, in which Mr. Spock would match wits with Captain Kirk and other crew members. Playing on the three-level chessboard is more dynamic and complex than playing on one flat board. Influences and power come from multiple directions, across, up, and down. This metaphor helps us to infuse human actors in systems thinking and speaks to the complexity of strategically leading school systems that comprise three levels within a larger environment that includes county, state, and federal policy makers. In contrast to Spock and Kirk's game, three-level chess for school reform positions the school district as an initiator and facilitator of positive change allied with

FIGURE 2.1 *Focal systems needed for the CPSF*

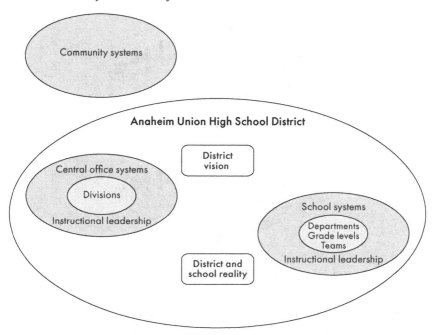

school and community systems against the status quo that opposes with inertia. (See figure 2.2.)

Level One: The School Site

Effective school leaders are strategic chess players at the site level and know how to optimize professional and decisional capital, terms introduced in Fullan's book *The Principal*. Fullan defines decisional capital as principals and other leaders having the skill and expertise to collaborate with stakeholders in their social networks as they make sound, site-level decisions in the best interest of students.[5]

School sites contain interdependent systems that include students, teachers, classified staff, parents, counselors, social workers, and administration. Teaching and learning are social processes that define schooling. Therefore, schools require a social-systemic approach to leadership for long-term stability and success.[6] Site leaders need to be strategic in integrating systems and

FIGURE 2.2 *Three-level chess*

Source: Wikimedia Commons, https://commons.wikimedia.org/wiki/File:Parallel_Worlds_Chess_levels.png.

structures so that individuals and groups (e.g., departments) do not operate in silos cut off from the larger social system. Fullan explains how adept leaders keep their schools aligned to a common vision, while Ackoff emphasizes the need to preserve choice and mitigate conflict.[7] Synthesizing the two, effective leaders develop social capital—access to expertise, assistance, and power within a social network—over time to ensure individual and group learning that is well informed and mutually reinforcing. Ideally, actions that leverage social capital are aligned to a common vision and common goals. In the process, decisional capital is expanded as expertise improves with action, reflection, and improved outcomes. When decisional capital and social capital are put to work, they can help leaders develop the school into a learning organization.

AUHSD works to ensure that the schools' visions are closely aligned with the district's vision, mission, and core values, as discussed in chapter 1. To establish and maintain such alignment requires teacher leaders' and administrators' ability to play three-level chess so that school sites and the district understand and respond to one another, with both considering the broader community.[8]

Level Two: The District

The district may struggle to achieve coherence across systems because the district office and divisions within it operate in silos. Their challenge is to break out of silos reinforced by daily operations, routines, and mind-sets. Just as in the case of schools, a social-systemic approach that enhances social and decisional capital is vital to sustain high-performing, interacting systems and to play three-level chess to win.

From the school leader's perspective, what would district leaders' effective play at level two on the chessboard look like? A functional relationship between site leaders and the district office (DO) is grounded in trust and open communication that embraces vulnerability and transparency, necessary conditions for learning and growing together. Principals, their administrative teams, and teacher leaders would see the DO as a supportive resource to help them achieve district and site visions. When principals, for example, share teaching and learning challenges with appropriate DO personnel, problems become "ours" rather than "yours" to solve. When site administrators view DO personnel as part of their own staff, then organizational learning at both levels—schools and DO—is possible. This perspective is achievable in AUHSD because there are substantial DO-based resources provided to sites in the form of coaches, curriculum specialists, technology, and professional learning. DO resources are mobilized to introduce and grow CPSF initiatives within schools. The resulting interdependence between the DO and sites helps to break down silos between schools and the DO and achieve greater cohesion. Social and decisional capital grow as challenges are addressed and problems are solved collaboratively.

Recognizing a possible history of failed implementation of unsupported mandates, DO leaders can repair past damage with a changed mind-set expressed as, "What are we doing to help the schools achieve district and school site visions?" For many DO personnel, this is a shift from ontological arrogance to ontological humility. Kofman explains ontological arrogance and humility with two archetypes—the controller and the learner. The arrogant (and often defensive) controller seeks to tell others what to do because the controller knows best. The more humble learner rejects the notion of one true reality and sees knowledge as emerging from a process of collaboration, reflection, and collective decision-making that is informed by evidence and multiple, diverse perspectives. Ontological arrogance can play out as a DO director telling principals what to do, principals giving marching orders to teachers, and teachers expecting students to follow commands such as "finish the worksheet." Ontological arrogance breeds fear—fear of failure, responsibility, or blame. Progress improving school and district performance starts with ontological humility that encourages collaborative learning throughout the organization by embracing diverse ideas, innovation, and tolerance for risk.[9] A learning organization depends on ontological humility.

A dilemma for DO leaders emerges when they try to give greater autonomy and flexibility to school sites. On one hand, relinquishing control from the center risks the possibility that any given school will veer from the district vision in pursuit of its own goals that could be inconsistent with that vision. On the other hand, too much control from the district office can stifle innovation and creative problem-solving. In previous research, superintendents articulated this dilemma as a choice between a *district of schools* in which educational experiences vary widely and a *school district* with a vision common to all school sites and policies and procedures in place to implement the vision.[10] A metaphor from business clarifies thinking about a balance between coherence and autonomy.

LEARNING FROM MCDONALD'S FRANCHISES. The franchise construct has been wildly successful for American businesses. The Egg McMuffin is an example from McDonald's in which innovation from a franchise adds substantial value to the entire organization. Herb Peterson, a McDonald's franchisee in California, "hatched" the Egg McMuffin as an innovation consistent with the overall company vision of fast service in a clean environment. Peterson applied new technology to a modified Eggs Benedict recipe, creating a menu item scalable for quick-service restaurants.[11] As of 2015, the Egg McMuffin had become so popular that McDonald's was responsible for purchasing approximately 5 percent of all the eggs produced in the United States.[12]

To encourage and develop more learners who embrace systems thinking, cohesion, and ontological humility, AUHSD has developed an organizational structure much akin to a franchise in which school sites are encouraged to innovate and take initiative in ways aligned to the vision, mission, and core values of the district. Schools have quite a lot of autonomy in pursuit of the

CPSF. This approach embodies DO ontological humility by preserving decision-making autonomy and choice at the school level with promising results such as the 5Cs and the Capstone project mentioned in chapter 1.

Before discussing level three, we want to return to the superintendent's dilemma of inadvertently creating a "district of schools," yet keeping the district together in a coherent manner might stifle innovation and lead to stagnation. Dilemmas by definition cannot be resolved, but they can be mitigated. In our case, we see the district monitoring and guiding schools to stay within the boundaries of the vision, mission, and values while allowing multiple paths toward the large goals, such as integrating twenty-first-century skills and technical skills.

Level Three: The Community

Elected school boards are a bridge between the community at large and the district and its schools. From that perspective, they operate at level two and level three practically simultaneously. They convey community aspirations (level three) as they determine school district policies and procedures (level two). Board members are responsible for policies that help to deliver the education their constituent families, colleges, and employers are seeking. They may also have direct access to community resources or the social capital to gain access. Boards work in concert with the superintendent whom they appoint to sustain quality and make necessary changes consistent with the policies and procedures they vote to put in place.

FOUNDATIONAL SCHOOL BOARD POLICY. Long before the pandemic, and even before Matsuda was elevated to superintendent, the board of trustees embraced the idea of educating the whole child. Members were committed to a comprehensive curriculum, including world languages, visual and performing arts, and CTE electives. Although previous superintendents were yoked to standardized tests, Matsuda worked with the AUHSD board to de-emphasize test scores as the primary indicator of educational success. He and the board understood that test scores were functioning as a sorting mechanism that worked against students' best interests. A singular focus on test scores stifled student voice and denied students opportunities to be successful in purposeful careers because such narrowly defined goals crowded out teaching both noncore content and twenty-first-century skills.

By 2015, the district no longer used test-based district benchmarks and state interim assessments. This change was a major reorientation away from the test-based No Child Left Behind and Race to the Top legislation that continues to dominate school district practices. It was driven, in part, by recognition that test-based criteria were unimportant to community employers and local government. Teachers agreed that a shift away from the narrow focus on tested outcomes was necessary to meet their students' needs while addressing what the community wanted from its schools as communicated through the school board. Yet, the status quo is a powerful adversary. Playing three-level chess means aligning community, board, DO, and school sites in a common purpose. The status quo uses test scores as proof of good schooling. Matsuda was frank with teacher leaders, explaining that if test scores declined, he wouldn't be superintendent for long. In a leap of faith, the district followed its North Star of educating the whole child, and teachers rose to the challenge. Test scores improved or stayed steady relative to comparable student populations from 2015 until today.[13]

Level three is where the school board, the superintendent, and the cabinet make most of their moves while mindful of level one and two moves and countermoves. Savvy principals, in turn, are aware of and responsive to level-three activity. Level-three influencers include local political leaders, businesses, nonprofit organizations, religious institutions, law enforcement, higher education institutions, parent leaders, alumni, and potential benefactors. Level-three play involves allying with individuals in multiple community institutions—seeking and encouraging their influence—to achieve educational goals. For schools and students to thrive, it is vital that district leaders, with assistance from principals and teacher leaders, know how to work productively with community leaders and ordinary folks.

Our discussion of level three is a practical application of an open systems perspective. By recognizing that the schools and district cannot and should not function as fortresses (closed systems) within the community, Matsuda and the AUHSD board position the district to take advantage of resources available from the community and beyond and protect themselves against external risks, otherwise known as bridging to resources and buffering against threats.[14] Successful bridging and buffering require communicating what the school district stands for and how it acts on its values as determined by the board and superintendent. This is three-level chess at its most complex because board member and superintendent incumbencies depend on the community understanding and supporting what the district is doing, and their credibility rests on the educational experience actually happening in schools and classrooms.

> ### Food for Thought 2.1
> Organizations theorist James D. Thompson argued long ago that organization leaders feel a need to pretend that their boundaries are solid in order to convey a sense of control. Does your school district deny the reality of external influences by pretending to be able to ignore them? Can you identify bridging and buffering actions that promote the district's vision?

Operationalizing Systems Thinking

Working from an understanding of a school's community context (level three) while applying that knowledge to shaping instruction in the classroom (level one) is aligned with what Senge has in mind when he describes systems thinking as seeing the whole and its parts. We use the three-level chess metaphor to operationalize Senge's systems thinking. When principals are simultaneously aware of district efforts to bridge to community resources and the degree to which students access opportunities inside and outside their classrooms, they are understanding their school's larger environment and its potential for improving education. Leaders capable of that kind of simultaneous thinking are adept at three-level chess. Figure 2.3 places key influencers at level three in our general model.

Communicating Vision Broadly and Deeply

When leaders align their work with vision, mission, and values, moving twenty or more schools in the same direction becomes possible. But knowledge of what drives the district to make major changes should be well understood by every teacher and staff member, parents, board members, and community partners. Communicating the meaning of and intent behind a

FIGURE 2.3 *AUHSD and its key influencers at level three*

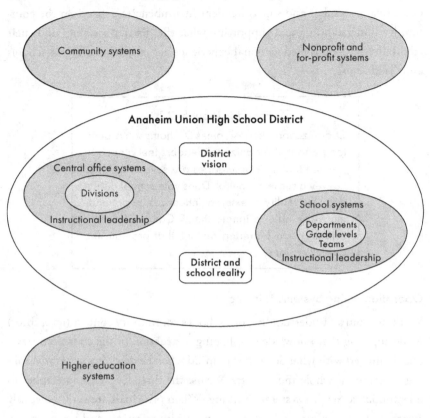

reform such as the CPSF is difficult. AUHSD turned to an international marketing firm to help translate the district's aspirations and values into a message that could be understood and supported by the community at large. A district teacher married to Ken Muench, the former chief marketing officer of Yum! Brands, provided a natural school-community link to strengthen play at level three.[15] Muench and a small team agreed to serve AUHSD pro bono over several months. They developed a branding strategy (something the district did not have previously) based on establishment of a "branded house" in favor of a "house of brands." Muench noted that nearly all school districts are vague entities, but individual schools are vivid in the minds of families and community members. He believed that AUHSD as an entire district needed a clearer identity in everyone's mind. Muench made the same point as the superintendents we referenced earlier—most school districts are branded as a district of schools rather than a school district. Matsuda and his cabinet agreed. Other than the superintendent and district office leaders and staff, almost no one identified with AUHSD. Most constituents instead identified with individual schools and often created mental models and assumptions about the district (and other schools) based on common knowledge. Elaborating on the branded house concept, Muench emphasized iconic names and images that communicate meaning and trust while engendering loyalty regardless of the individual product.

Superintendent Matsuda found that when presented with the branded house concept, the AUHSD executive team recognized that a clear district brand could be an effective tool in three-level chess. Muench helped the team adopt the goal to become an iconic name in public education that stands for high-quality teaching and learning that serve students' needs in every school and program.

After studying surrounding districts, private schools, and charter schools, the Muench team found that AUHSD was known for providing an authentic, distinctive educational experience. They introduced the tagline "Unlimited You" to elevate the branded house concept and market AUHSD distinctiveness. Figure 2.4 is the now ubiquitous logo that conveys AUHSD's commitment to students and families.

Having a distinct brand with the recognizable mortar board logo communicates aspirations, values, and consistency vertically through all levels of the chessboard, as seen in figure 2.5.

FIGURE 2.4 *AUHSD tagline and logo*

Systems Thinking Summary

Seeing schools and districts as systems within other systems helps to explain the complexity built into education and into the process of trying to change educational purpose and function. It is important to be clear about our use of language. If school districts and the process of education were merely complicated, we would know all the relevant variables and reduce the problem of educational improvement to manipulating the right ones. But schools and districts not only are complicated, but are also *complex systems*. Complexity is generated by ambiguity—what cannot be known in the present—inherent in the educational process and our own cognitive limitations for understanding what is happening in the moment.[16]

The three-level chessboard is our metaphor for leading multiple systems within and outside the school district. The process of generating change on three levels simultaneously seems daunting. Nevertheless, adapting to the three-level chess game of schooling, instead of avoiding it, can produce dramatic results. Three-level chess is an apt metaphor for systems thinking because it requires simultaneous knowledge of each chess piece's position in

FIGURE 2.5 *Visibility of "Unlimited You"*

HUMAN RELATIONS ESSENTIAL TO POSITIVE CHANGE

> [S]ystems thinking... shows that small, well-focused actions can sometimes produce significant, enduring improvements, if they're in the right place. Systems thinkers refer to this principle as "leverage."
>
> Tackling a difficult problem is often a matter of seeing where high leverage lies, a change which—with a minimum of effort—would lead to lasting, significant improvement.[17]

In Senge's general discussion of organizational complexity, he emphasizes that small actions ripple throughout organizations to generate the change we are seeking, taking advantage of interconnected systems. The quotation that leads this section explains the importance of small actions defined by Senge as "trim tabs."[18] Trim tabs are small portions of ships' rudders or airplane wings that create leverage that changes the direction of these massive objects moving against immense resistance in water or air.[19] The analogy works well for school districts that are often compared to aircraft carriers when authors attempt to explain how difficult they are to change. AUHSD has leveraged trim tabs in the form of people in positions throughout the district. Their effectiveness depends on both their skill sets and their interactions with other professionals. Human relations matter. They help to change the district systemically, including the multiple subsystems within it.

Trim Tab Power

Matsuda deliberately works to create positions with potential trim tab power and nurture their influence. For example, there are teachers at every school who are released from teaching two class periods who are called "5Cs coaches" because their role is to help teachers integrate the 5Cs into their daily teaching. The 5Cs coaches, acting in their teacher leadership role, make incremental changes working with teachers one-on-one and through group professional learning to improve practice. Over time, small adjustments that 5Cs coaches make with individual teachers add up to a changed learning experience for large groups of students. One person—one trim tab—can make a substantial difference in the life of the school.

Matsuda expands the trim tab concept by asking principals and other administrators to learn who has influence—who is a trim tab—at their sites. Trim tab people can either help to align the school with the vision and mission of the district or try to guide people and the organization in the opposite direction, undermining leadership and cohesion. They often use private, informal opportunities to play their part at level one of three-level chess. It is the responsibility of school site leaders to channel and motivate trim tab action in a direction consistent with the CPSF and district and school visions, while neutralizing the opposite.

Trim tab leaders working from the district (curriculum specialists) and school sites (5Cs coaches) have been essential to getting a critical mass of teachers to reflect on their instruction and apply the 5Cs that constitute the core of twenty-first-century skills. When the 5Cs are prominent in instruction, students have opportunities to explore the ideas that develop into their sense of purpose and find their unique voice that expresses who they are and what they aspire to become. The 5Cs are simple in concept and, through intentional implementation, can generate a large effect on student outcomes when coupled with other opportunities. Thus, as Senge imagines, the efforts of 5Cs coaches ripple through educational systems within AUHSD—classrooms, schools, and the district collectively—and move educational purposes, actions, and outcomes goals toward the CPSF. When site and district leaders employ trim tab people consistent with vision, mission, and values, they are generating coherence throughout the district and its subsystems.[20]

Trim Tabs Within Community Systems

As helpful as trim tabs may be in making organizational change, they are not sufficient for realizing a vision as large and multifaceted as that embodied in the CPSF. Recall from chapter 1 that Matsuda was inspired by student action in the community protest against police shootings. He was encouraged by Tom Tait, Anaheim mayor at the time, who responded to the students in a manner that made their voice important, as he and the city council changed policing policies and practices.

Our perspective on interacting systems expands when we think about ways in which municipalities, their departments, and the people within them might interact with the nested systems inside school districts—the district office, schools, and classrooms. Tait's willingness as the chief executive of the City of Anaheim to help students air their grievances allowed the students to articulate their sense of the opportunity deficits in their community that were the root cause of pain and protest. With the anguish of police shootings as the backdrop in 2012, mothers spoke of the trauma of losing their sons at the hands of police while still young students. As mothers pleaded for peace in the community, their children expressed the frustration of low-income Latino youth lacking career preparation and meaningful job opportunities. Mayor Tait's interest in youth development and his ambition to improve the City of Anaheim as a community placed him in the role of vital trim tab for initiating change within AUHSD.

The vivid experiences of the summer and fall of 2012 demonstrated to Matsuda and others the potential in forging systemic relationships among the school district, city hall, and nonprofit and for-profit enterprises. With these systems pulling in the same direction to nurture the community's youth, high school graduates' skills, knowledge, and dispositions would be enhanced so that they could be ready for meaningful work after high school. At the same time, the community would be strengthened by AUHSD providing motivated, capable employees for a wide range of economic endeavors. Creating partnerships with additional trim tab people across systems would strengthen the entire community—K–12 schools, higher education, municipal government, and private enterprise. This was the vision beginning to take shape before Matsuda became superintendent.

Permeable Boundaries Create Trim Tab Opportunities

Motivated by the example of students spontaneously accessing political resources from the mayor's office, Matsuda has bridged to resources available in several sectors in Orange County—colleges and universities, for-profit and nonprofit enterprises, and local government. Partnerships with multiple systems that heretofore lacked explicit relationships with the school district are vital to the CPSF agenda. They provide students with broader knowledge of the workplace, the community, and educational opportunities beyond high school.[21]

The benefits from taking advantage of the open systems nature of education organizations are obvious, but there are constant threats as well. State financing rules—namely a reliance on average daily attendance to determine district funding—threaten AUHSD's budget as student enrollment declines for reasons that have little to do with educational choice. Making positive change is more difficult under conditions of financial constraint. In the specific case of AUHSD's pursuit of the CPSF, the capacity to cultivate and manage multiple relationships throughout Orange County and make those meaningful to students and teachers requires personnel expenditures threatened by potential revenue shortfalls. Matsuda is acting through local state representatives to try to buffer against—mitigate or eliminate—threats that may materialize in coming years. At the same time, the district is aggressive in bridging to resources through human relations–based outreach to organizations and obtaining grants to fund programs.

Bridging and buffering are behaviors that recognize interdependent systems influences. It is unusual for education leaders to see the open systems nature of their schools and districts as an advantage. More commonly, outside influences are seen as threats, and leaders tend to try to close off their systems in response.[22] Seeing the possibilities in trim tab people and comprehending the nature of schools and districts as systems operating within a larger context of multiple additional systems is a rather heavy cognitive lift, yet it is only part of the picture. Analyzing the opportunities and constraints of the status quo in order to change it requires courage and self-discipline. A major aspiration of the CPSF is to "elevate student voice and purpose"—a tectonic shift in the educational status quo in AUHSD and most US school districts. Such a change requires that the district's internal systems engage in learning and that the district initiate and sustain learning processes with external systems as a set of moves in three-level chess.

Food for Thought 2.2

Name the three most powerful systems in your school district's community. Are they ready, willing, and eager to sign on to the vision? What actions have been taken to solicit their support? What might they gain in return?

ORGANIZATIONAL LEARNING: A MAJOR CHALLENGE

Vision and mission statements help to guide AUHSD through uncertainty and ambiguity. They clarify educators' purpose and help to channel decision-making. As the district's North Star, they describe the ideal toward which the district and its schools and partners are striving.

Creative Tension

> The juxtaposition of vision (what we want) and a clear picture of current reality (where we are relative to what we want) generates what we call "creative tension": a force to bring them together caused by the natural tendency of tension to seek resolution. The essence of personal mastery is learning how to generate and sustain creative tension in our lives.[23]

Moving the district forward toward its aspirations—its vision—is a daily process that works slowly. We imagine individuals within their systems and subsystems considering the vision and their daily work relative to that vision. Being in the middle of a change period, most are likely to find a gap between the goals and objectives of the vision and their daily work, or what Senge calls their *reality*. As mentioned in chapter 1, Matsuda emphasizes Senge's notion of creative tension as he encourages district leaders to pull their reality closer to the district vision. Grappling with creative tension is not a process that leaders come to naturally, possibly because doing so involves some degree of admission that their work is not living up to ideals. If anything, natural tendencies move in the other direction, pulling the vision toward reality with statements such as, "We're already doing that." A learning organization deliberately and explicitly surfaces creative tension intent on changing the status quo to bring reality closer to vision. Focal creative tension is represented in the center of figure 2.6.

Kofman further specifies creative tension in his discussion of three dimensions of business: "the impersonal, task, or 'It'; the interpersonal, relationship, or 'We'; and the personal, self, or 'I.'"[24] The impersonal It is an organization's ability to achieve its vision, mission, and core values. Impersonal success is the existential reality of the organization—without it, the organization may not survive. For too long, too many school districts have allowed their It to be defined by federal and state policy makers who have defined achievement

FIGURE 2.6 *Creative tension at the center of change in AUHSD*

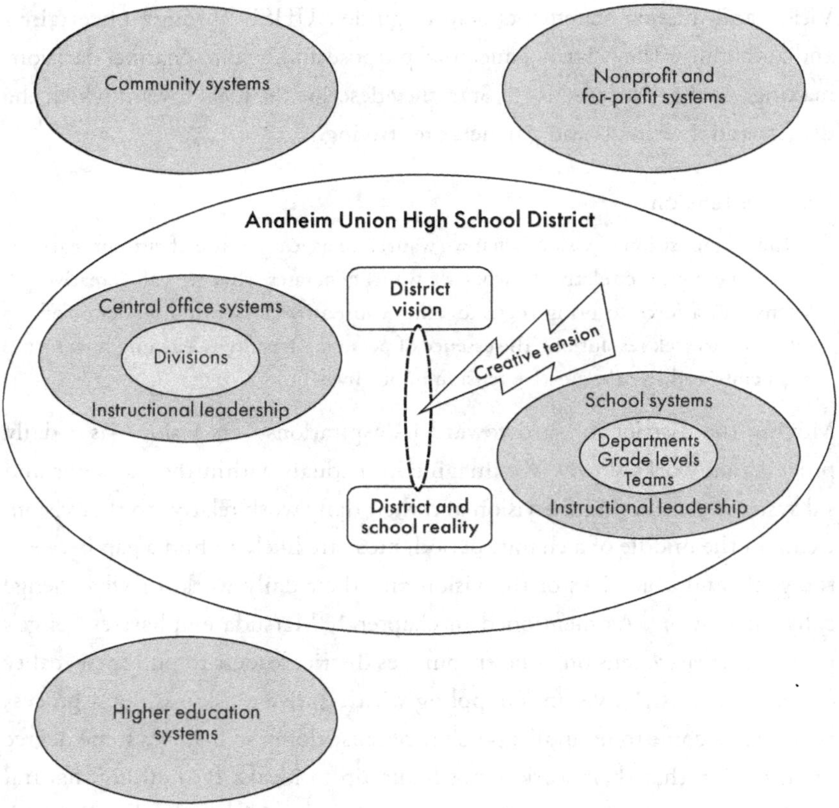

gaps and academic and career readiness in terms of scores on standardized tests and other metrics that miss what is most important in students' lives. Absent from most educational systems, we believe, is organizing in support of We and I aligned to vision, mission, and core values that address students' needs. Clearly stating what It the district is pursuing is insufficient. District leaders must understand the individual and interpersonal aspirations, needs, and limitations of all stakeholders in order to achieve the larger vision because it is the *people* within systems that make them work. For AUHSD, the It is encompassed in a school system that lives up to Unlimited You, while We and I are cultivated through instructional leadership and professional learning.[25]

Strengthening the We and I in pursuit of the It is a big part of the education leader's job. Senge explains that for leaders to be learners—both literally and in the sense of Kofman's ontologically humble leader—requires personal mastery. "Organizations learn through individuals who learn. Individual learning does not guarantee organizational learning, but without it, no learning occurs."[26] Half of personal mastery is understanding who I am as an individual, where I stand with peers, and how my work is related to the overall purpose of the school and district. The second half is an open-mindedness to discovering how the world really is. For example, a teacher examines student work as evidence of teaching effectiveness. This discovery—learning—is how creative tension is generated because it shows us the difference between vision and reality. The essence of personal mastery is sustaining an emotional equilibrium while understanding how and why my work must improve. The organizational learning analogue is knowing the ways in which the status quo must change and taking steps to do so.[27]

Kofman explains the importance of personal mastery:

> Personal success is critical . . . If people are not happy in their jobs, they will not remain engaged, they will not last as productive employees. They will not quit formally, but they will quit emotionally. In order to obtain energy from its employees, the organization needs to provide them with opportunities for physical, emotional, mental, and spiritual well-being. If an organization's people do not experience this well-being, it will fail.[28]

We touch on some of the fundamental affective characteristics of educators involved in reform in the sections that follow and elaborate on how to foster well-being in chapter 5.

Change: Resistance and Motivation

Seeing opportunities in interconnected systems and mobilizing individuals to exploit those opportunities tend to assume forward motion and success if the right steps are followed. Such a view is simplistic because individuals within systems have widely varying skills, knowledge, and motivation. Ackoff recognizes the importance of considering individual motivations within social systems.[29] There are feedback and influence loops that connect individuals in social networks that exist inside schools, districts, and the numerous systems in the community with which they interact. Trim tab people, working for change or defending the status quo, affect organizational direction through these loops. Understanding the persistent nature of the status quo and the ways in which that persistence makes positive change challenging begins with recognizing individuals' resistance to change.

Lewin explained organizational dynamics as the interplay between individuals and the systems in which they find themselves. For our purposes, the most important idea from Lewin is that people do not resist change; they *resist being changed*.[30] A common example helps explain why. When unions and school district administrations negotiate contracts, they start from basic interests that differ. The union side likely seeks rules that ensure equal treatment of bargaining unit members and minimize administration discretion to make demands on teachers' time. The administration, for its part, seeks to minimize the number of rules and maximize discretion in the name of maintaining and improving the quality of instruction and leadership prerogative. We can assume, however, that the teacher union also seeks instructional quality, and the administration wants all teachers treated fairly. If either side proposes a change to the negotiated agreement, the opposing side is inclined to resist, despite a recognition of common interests, because they feel an attempt by others to force their constituents to change. If, on the other hand, the two sides can discover their common interests together, they may be more inclined to initiate change in a collaborative manner.

Lewin used the vivid metaphor of an object frozen in place to represent an initial position or the status quo. He claimed that change wouldn't happen without "unfreezing" first. It is only when people are in the process of unfreezing that they are open to learning and can make change within systems. Senge built on Lewin's conception of change resistance by arguing that examining creative tension leads to unfreezing. Once change (or movement, as Lewin saw it) happens, refreezing will occur in the form of a new status quo. We modify Lewin and Weisbord a bit in figure 2.7 to show how learning fits into Lewin's original conception.[31]

This simple change model becomes complicated in the unfreezing stage. For any given individual to unfreeze and make a change likely requires that person to understand *why* the change is a good idea and *how to* make the change. A learning disposition (ontological humility), motivation to change, and the skills and knowledge required to change are necessary and mutually supporting. Weisbord provides plain language practical steps needed for unfreezing:

FIGURE 2.7 *A conception of change as a process of unfreezing and learning*

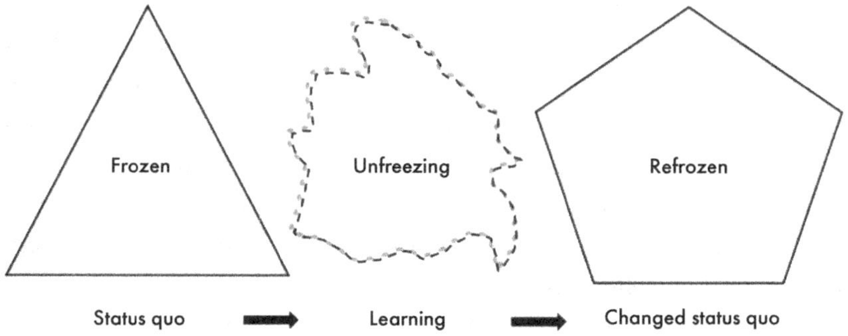

Frozen — Unfreezing — Refrozen

Status quo ➡ Learning ➡ Changed status quo

If stored up stuff [unresolved process issues] could be got out in the open, if people could express their resistances and skepticism, if undiscussable topics could be talked about, energy would be released. People would become aware of their own contributions to their problems. The blockages would be removed . . . and new behavior would emerge—a possibility that might accelerate through skill training. Unfrozen people would redo strategy, policy, procedure, relationships, and norms more to their liking. Implementing new action plans would move the system, and reinforcing mechanisms . . . would refreeze the system into more functional patterns.[32]

Weisbord, a business consultant with a love for academics, simplified and clarified Lewin's work by explaining that unfreezing is a process of showing organization participants with data and open discussion that their systems are not achieving stated goals. This knowledge helps to unfreeze them so that they can move to new processes that then become institutionalized. Think of the revised status quo as a reformed organization frozen into a new set of operations that better serve the vision. AUHSD's conference in Portland described at the beginning of this chapter was an unfreezing effort intended to invigorate AUHSD staff's implementation of and support for the CPSF.

The change process is neither simple nor easy largely because *individuals* need to make the changes the system seeks. In chapter 6 we discuss ways in which professional learning can serve as an unfreezing process.

Systems That Learn

Senge, Kofman, Ackoff, and Lewin all take different paths toward organizational improvement that converge on the concept of learning—both individual and organizational. Understanding individual learning is straightforward for educators, but figuring out how a system or organization learns is not. Argyris and Schön provide an important foundation for how Senge, Kofman, and Ackoff think about change. Argyris and Schön imagine two kinds of systemic or organizational learning, single and double loop.[33] Single-loop learning examines flaws in status quo implementation and provides immediate fixes without challenging the established order, while double-loop learning finds flaws in the status quo itself. These flaws are the gaps between the real and ideal generated by a new and compelling vision.

Addressing the gap between the real and ideal—wrestling with creative tension—generates long-term solutions in the form of changing the status quo toward the new vision. Single-loop learning *improves* how the status quo functions, while double-loop learning *changes* the status quo. AUHSD's double-loop learning consists of changing the status quo from pursuit of higher test scores to finding and pursuing more meaningful indicators of student accomplishment within technical skills, twenty-first-century skills, and elevating youth voice and purpose.[34] Major school reform embodied in the CPSF cannot be achieved through single-loop learning. Knowing the root causes of status quo flaws—the reasons those flaws exist and persist—provides change targets. Ultimately, whatever solutions are chosen should be those that mitigate or eliminate root causes and bring reality closer to vision.[35] Figure 2.8 completes our model that embraces systems thinking and organizational learning by including double-loop learning and instructional leadership (discussed in the next section).

Learning will happen separately in the various systems that make up the network that provides education to students. Changing the fundamental educational experience for students will not happen from the district acting alone. Remembering the open systems perspective, political and economic threats from beyond district boundaries must be countered by accessing political, social, and economic resources in the community. Bridging to resources likely involves organizational learning within the external systems that support the school district, that is, other systems may also need to change their status quo to help achieve district goals. A mundane yet vivid example follows.

PUTTING COLLEGE TEXTBOOKS IN STUDENTS' HANDS. In AUHSD's pursuit of the CPSF, one very specific example of double-loop organizational learning

FIGURE 2.8 *Double-loop learning within systems thinking*

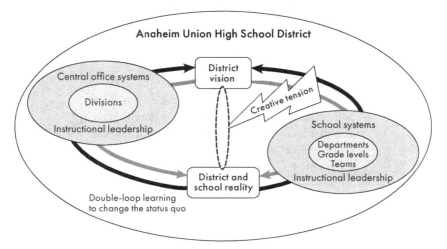

within an external entity comes from community colleges' partnerships with the district to provide dual-enrollment courses in which students earn both high school and college credit. Professors in the colleges are accustomed to selecting their own textbooks and reading materials and changing sources when it suits them. This practice is incompatible with dual enrollment because source materials used by high school students must be approved by the school board. Both the school district and the community colleges (there are two that partner closely with AUHSD) have the incentives and intent to increase dual-enrollment numbers, but changing the status quo textbook adoption process at community colleges was needed to bring dual-enrollment outcomes into alignment with aspirations. When the community colleges agreed to three-year textbook adoptions for dual-enrollment courses and submitted recommended texts to the school district for approval, the operational status quo was changed, and dual enrollment emerged as an opportunity for many more students.[36]

The shift in textbook procedures is a clear example of individuals working together to change a small procedure with a large effect—a trim tab. This micro-level change fuels persistence to a bachelor's degree for low-income and other student groups that typically struggle to complete community college programs and graduate with a BA within six years of high school graduation.

Earning college credit gives these students an important educational and financial leg up when they graduate from high school having completed a portion of their general education requirements.[37]

> **Food for Thought 2.3**
> How willing is your district to examine the rules and norms that hold the status quo in place? How does this level of commitment to changing the status quo affect efforts to improve the educational experience?

INSTRUCTIONAL LEADERSHIP

Systems thinking and the learning that potentially happens within it helps us understand how to change the status quo, but for education organizations such as schools and districts, it offers no specific guidance on aspects of the status quo that need changing. Instructional leadership provides the focus for learning within educational systems because the most important gaps between vision and reality are about teaching and learning. Instructional leadership tools are needed to move the district from test score focus to purposeful life focus. As the label suggests, it's about leading learning—for students, teachers, parents, and the community.

Instructional leadership takes place on many levels throughout the systems that make up the school district. The general leadership challenge is to ensure that instruction is being led consistently within and across systems in terms of instructional values, processes, and outcomes. We demonstrate how this works by starting with the central office and then moving to schools, teacher collaborative teams, and classrooms. We recognize that school districts come in many shapes and sizes. To focus our discussion, we use the AUHSD perspective of a medium-sized district with resources commensurate with spending approximately $15,000 per student during 2022–2023. Readers can adapt what we describe to their own contexts.

Central Office: In Support of Schools

Our experience with public school systems is fraught with tension between central offices and school sites. An us-versus-them mentality is easily developed from both sides. While central office departments are concerned with monitoring schools' implementation of programs and practices, principals and teachers often jealously guard school and classroom autonomy. AUHSD strives to overcome this kind of status quo thinking by focusing the district office and the school sites on CPSF goals and objectives, while allowing schools autonomy to create and nurture the classroom practices that pursue agreed-on goals and objectives on a daily basis. It is a dance between the district office and the sites, between the central corporation and the franchisee. Helping leaders at various levels work together to achieve instructional goals happens when central office personnel provide resources to schools that support the kind of instruction communicated through the district's vision, mission, and core values. Two examples of AUHSD programs squarely focused on achieving CPSF goals help to illustrate the point.[38]

DEMOCRACY SCHOOLS. The phrase *civic-minded* appears in the AUHSD mission and *equity and justice* and *strengthen democracy* appear in the core values. Among the district's curriculum specialists (teachers on special assignment based at the DO serving all the schools), Reuben Patino has committed himself to helping schools initiate and maintain the Democracy Schools program as one means of operationalizing the civil society–oriented, democratic values embedded in the mission and core values of the district. He engages AUHSD teachers in professional learning to foster democratic values in classrooms and to help students voice their aspirations in civic engagement. Patino's instructional leadership in this area empowers classroom teachers to lead civic engagement instruction at their sites. Students achieve the civic engagement and voice and purpose goals embedded in the CPSF when they take part in Democracy Schools instruction. The State of California has a program that has recognized fifteen of the twenty-one AUHSD schools as Democracy Schools.[39]

CAPSTONE PROJECTS. As described in chapter 1, the Capstone project is intended to be an opportunity for students to showcase their learning in the areas of technical skills and twenty-first-century skills, with particular emphasis on their developing capacity to employ the 5Cs. In 2021–2022, the district office communicated the expectation that all of the district's schools would follow Savanna High School's lead and institute Capstone experiences that are grounded in student-generated portfolios. Schools were given latitude (autonomy and choice that opens the door to leadership opportunity and innovation) to design Capstones that were age and context appropriate. As they worked on their designs, Mike Switzer, an English curriculum specialist who was deeply involved in the original Capstone design, created a Capstone playbook to assist teachers and administrators in creating critical elements such as performance task assessments, portfolio guidelines, and Capstone interviews at the end of the year.

We recognize that from the two examples given above, it can seem as though the district is imposing new tasks on school sites. In a way it is, but these tasks help turn the schools toward CPSF goals. Thus, the curriculum specialists are directly involved in showing teachers and school leaders *what* the CPSF looks like in practice and *how* to engage in the kind of teaching and learning that is emblematic of CPSF goals. Ideally, they provide productive channels for creative tension that bring reality closer in line with vision.

The 5Cs coaches introduced in our discussion of three-level chess are essential instructional leaders based in school sites and coordinated from the DO. These teachers on special assignment are purposely kept in the classroom for three-fifths of their contract to help them stay grounded in instruction. The two-fifths released provides time for one-on-one coaching with teachers and leadership of professional learning for the school. The 5Cs coaches are a bridge between the district office and the schools because their own professional development and general learning are planned and implemented by a DO director, while in their day-to-day work, they are in close contact with principals and engage with teachers at their schools.

In their coaching and professional learning roles, 5Cs coaches build on resources made available by curriculum specialists to help teachers individually and collectively embed the 5Cs in their instruction, foster civic-mindedness and democracy, and generate performance task assessments for the Capstone project. When they work effectively, they help their school to access and use resources provided by the district. They are uniquely positioned to mitigate an us-versus-them mentality and help their school-based system work in harmony and toward common goals with the district system.

School Sites: In Support of Teachers

We assume that principals lead learning in their schools. They don't do this work alone, of course, but they are essential members of teams that shape teachers' professional learning. Their instructional leadership, both direct and indirect, is second only to teachers in their impact on student achievement.[40] We believe that principals facilitating teams of administrators and teacher leaders all functioning in instructional leadership roles provide the strongest structure to focus and energize professional learning that serves the district's vision, mission, and core values. Examples of school site teams helping to lead instruction follow.

PRINCIPAL AND SCHOOL SITE CABINET. Configurations of the administrative team are likely to vary across schools and districts. In AUHSD, the administrative team we have in mind is called the cabinet.[41] The principal's cabinet consists of the principal, assistant principals, 5Cs coach, lead counselor, and other teacher leaders the principal might appoint. The principal determines how the cabinet will engage with teachers in instructional areas, with the 5Cs coach playing their role as described above. Beyond communicating with departments, the cabinet has a collective responsibility to:

- Be informed and involved with professional development provided by the central office.
- Work with the school site professional learning team to shape the school's entire professional development experience.
- Identify and address the various professional learning needs of departments, teacher teams, and individuals.
- Engage in professional learning alongside teachers to understand how curriculum and pedagogy are taking shape and to convey that understanding by their presence and participation.[42]

It is the primary responsibility of the cabinet to create and implement professional learning that improves instruction consistent with the district's instructional goals.

Professional learning team. Principals provide guidance to their professional learning teams made up of teacher leaders. Typical professional learning teams (PL team) include one or two members of the school site cabinet, the 5Cs coach, and department heads. The PL team helps the school site cabinet to refine and design teachers' professional development experiences based on what they know from their other roles in the school. The 5Cs coaches are often delegated the task of organizing and implementing the professional learning designed by the PL team.

Department chairs. Teachers in these roles are expected to step up as peer leaders within their departments to engage in one-on-one and collective support for teaching and learning initiatives. They are required to be informed through monthly district meetings, membership on the PL team, or in collaboration with the 5Cs coach.

Influencers. These are informal teacher leaders within all AUHSD schools. They may have served in teacher leader roles already described but are not now in such roles. They lead by example, and their work is often showcased within their school and across the district. They may serve on the PL team and on various committees, but their full-time role is as a classroom teacher.

Summary

AUHSD strives to develop instructional leadership capacity through the DO and school sites working in partnership. Many individuals serving on multiple, sometimes overlapping teams engage in instructional leadership across schools throughout the district every day. Instructional leadership and the professional learning that results is vital to energizing organizational learning and changing the direction of instruction in AUHSD. To achieve a coherent system, these individuals and the teams they serve require regular, sustained communication that runs from schools to the DO and back again. All the instructional leaders who play roles at the central office and within school sites are essential to keeping the district's schools and classrooms moving in the same direction and mitigating the us-versus-them beliefs that bubble up in most school districts. These are the individuals who are supported by the district and, in turn, improve the systems that make up the school district. Through their daily work leading instruction, they propel the district toward the changed vision for secondary education.

OUR FRAMEWORK FOR CHANGING THE DIRECTION OF SECONDARY EDUCATION

Implementation of the CPSF is guided by a four-step theory of action: (1) clarify and communicate the district's vision, mission, and core values; (2) identify interdependent systems—both inside and outside the school district—that generate students' educational experiences; (3) use the creative tension generated by the difference between aspirations embedded in the vision and mission and current reality to motivate change (unfreezing); (4) engage in double-loop organizational learning through instructional leadership that changes the status quo to closely align outcomes with aspirations. This theory of action is explained graphically in figure 2.8.

Systems thinking is complex, and organizational learning is slow and meandering. These approaches require a great deal of attention and focus over a long time and a willingness to make course corrections. For these reasons and more, it is far more common for education leaders to engage in single-loop learning: efforts to fix immediate problems while keeping schools and districts running smoothly. Single-loop actions are attractive because they yield results in the very short term. Such efforts may not be long-lasting, however, because the problems they are intended to address are perpetuated by the status quo. Double-loop learning as we describe in this chapter changes what Argyris and Schön call "governing variables"—the rules, norms, and behaviors that are the major components of the status quo.[43] We have mentioned an important such governing variable that we reiterate here: test scores as the sole measure of student achievement. AUHSD has changed that particular rule with the CPSF. No longer preeminent, test scores are but one de-emphasized measure, with the 5Cs, dual enrollment, and civic engagement as a few among many other indicators of students' path toward a purposeful life. Discovering and changing the governing variables that matter most is an important theme for the rest of the book. We use the framework developed in this chapter to explain the practical steps and challenges of implementing the CPSF and like-minded education reforms.

A LOOK AHEAD

Chapter 3 begins the reader's journey through the CPSF experience from the perspective of AUHSD students, because the CPSF is *for the benefit of students*. Readers will recognize similarities and differences with the student populations they serve, thus bringing a strong dose of reality to the story we are telling. Another part of this reality is that important segments of a school district's constituents will be invested in the status quo. Changing the status quo is easily perceived as depriving one or more groups of resources, thereby generating resistance to change. To say that what we are doing is "in the best interest of students" is insufficient. Becoming familiar with the diverse student population served by AUHSD helps us to understand the inevitable resistance to change and how to work with it.

TAKING STOCK

The framework we present in this chapter is intended to demonstrate major systems interaction that make positive change possible. We suggest that you consider these essential questions:

1. What are the most important systems within and outside your district?
2. How well are these systems functioning together?
3. How would you describe the most important creative tension?

Figure 2.9 is a template you can use to answer these questions for your local context.

FIGURE 2.9 *A systems thinking template for your school district*

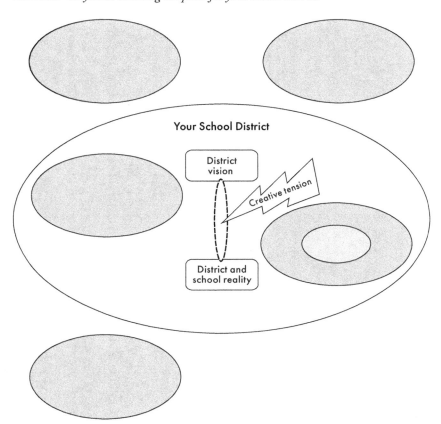

CHAPTER 3

ADDRESSING EVERY STUDENT'S STORY, FOSTERING AGENCY

> As I began my transition into the superintendent role, Adela Cruz, the district director of mental health, arranged for me to have dinner with Abby, a seventeen-year-old homeless student who was a rising senior at Magnolia High School. After dinner with Abby and her family at an Anaheim restaurant, I escorted them to the temporary homeless shelter in a large Santa Ana church where they were staying at the time. Reality set in as I looked around the church gym that was "home" for the night for Abby's family and about fifty other families. What struck me was that although they were sleeping on the gym floor, the children, especially the little ones, were playing and laughing as if they were in their own home. Abby needed to get up at 5 a.m. each day to take two buses on a ninety-minute journey to high school. After school, she routinely took a bus to a local library to complete her homework on a computer. In the evening, Abby would locate her family and take her final bus of the day to wherever they were.
>
> —MICHAEL MATSUDA, SUPERINTENDENT

SECONDARY SCHOOLS ARE INSTITUTIONS that expect students to conform to a 180-day calendar and daily schedule based on both agriculture (school out of session during planting, cultivation, and harvest seasons) and the mass production industry (time schedules and their enforcement with bells or chimes).[1] They were not designed with homeless children in mind, or children with any other life challenges for that matter. Children have been expected to adapt to school life or face the consequences of failure. Abby is a resilient survivor we'll share a bit more about later. Because of conditions beyond their control, not all students are as strong.

Through the doorway of twenty-first-century skills embodied in the 5Cs, AUHSD strives to strengthen students' affective skills so that they are more resilient with respect to life's challenges and inspired to learn technical skills at their highest potential. To make sense of strategies such as the 5Cs and Democracy Schools or the centrality of phrases such as "elevating student voice and purpose," we want to make clear to readers who the students are on multiple dimensions. Educating the whole child in the twenty-first century means adapting to their identities and life experiences, their intersectionality. Describing the student population's vivid characteristics demonstrates to leaders and other educators the degree to which AUHSD students are similar to and different from students in their own districts and schools. Researchers will learn the demographics of the school district and understand the context that is so important for determining which actions cause what outcomes. Learning the student population's needs is the first step toward shaping district programming, educational approaches, and resources to improve postgraduation prospects for all students.

AUHSD students attend schools based on family residence, with several notable exceptions. Homeless families are permitted under state law to send their children to one school regardless of where they might be located at any given time. This is what allowed Abby to have a consistent high school experience. AUHSD has a magnet school with grades 7–12, the Oxford Academy, for which residence location is irrelevant. Students who wish to participate in a specific career pathway may attend a high school different from the one in their attendance area. Independent studies, virtual programs, and the continuation high school are also not residence based.[2] Knowing that the vast majority of students attend their neighborhood junior high or high school provides an important frame to make sense of the district's demographic patterns.

AUHSD is remarkably homogenous in some unexpected ways. We begin an exploration of demographics with socioeconomics.

MOST FAMILIES STRUGGLE WITH BASIC NEEDS

Overshadowed by the glitter and romance of Disneyland and other tourist attractions, poverty is prevalent in AUHSD schools. In the last three school years, the percentage of district students classified as low income ranged from over 70 percent in 2019–2020 to over 74 percent in 2021–2022. In the same period, enrollment in the district declined by 1,429 students as job loss and the COVID-19 pandemic pushed families to lower-rent locations.

Today, AUHSD has over 1,650 homeless students attending junior high and high schools. Abby was just one of many. When community leaders welcomed Matsuda as superintendent, he shared the spotlight with Abby. It was the first time that a superintendent had put homeless students front and center as an educational priority. Abby tearfully thanked her teachers, many of whom knew her situation and were flexible when it came to homework and tests. Against all odds, Abby graduated from the one high school she attended, earning a C average. She subsequently enrolled in community college. Her example continues to inspire Matsuda and AUHSD educators to know every student by name and story.

Abby's story and other stories about extreme personal challenges absorbed Matsuda's attention. Since 2015, the district has emphasized knowing students as individuals so that no one would feel anonymous in their large, fast-paced secondary schools. This short phrase "know every student by name and story" is emblematic of creating a sense of belonging and more inclusive culture in classrooms and schools. Knowing every story especially applies to the marginalized, underserved, and often ignored students such as multilingual learners, students with special needs, foster youth students, and homeless students. In the spirit of understanding who at least a portion of students in AUHSD are, we present Abby and others in this chapter to illustrate some of the signature challenges many students face.

In 2019, Assistant Principal Ruben Calleros from Anaheim High School shared a powerful story about Axel, who at the time was a ninth grader. Axel was teased because of a prosthetic leg, which caused him to limp badly. One day in his math class, Axel was ridiculed and a fight erupted, causing Axel to be sent to Mr. Calleros. At that time, Axel's deteriorating classroom behavior was part of a downward trajectory that included declining grades. Calleros told Axel's story this way:

> *Axel came to my office to let me know what happened in the class and broke down in tears as he told me the story of his amputated leg. Prior to him coming to the US when he was about twelve years old, Axel was kidnapped in Guatemala and*

the kidnappers asked for ransom money. According to Axel, this was pretty common in Guatemala. He said his family did not have money to pay the ransom. As a consequence, the kidnappers beat him, poured acid on his leg, and then committed a more horrific act. They shot him once in the leg and left him for dead on the side of the road. He was fortunate enough that someone found him; however, his leg was so damaged it had to be amputated.

As Axel told me this story, he cried multiple times. I reminded him that he did not have to share with me, but I wanted to understand. I couldn't help but cry with him as he told it.

We talked about the incident [fight] that occurred in his class, and I told Axel that it would be addressed. Axel was concerned that the students were going to see him as a "snitch." I assured him that was not going to happen. In the process of our conversation, Axel was reflective and he asked if he could tell his story to the class. Axel figured that might help everyone understand his situation and just leave him alone. I was apprehensive at first, but after speaking with our social worker, admin team, and Axel's parents, we decided he should go ahead.

The next week, Axel told his story to his math class, and it hit hard. You could hear a pin drop in that room as he spoke. Subsequently, his story reached Superintendent Matsuda, who, with help from some AUHSD partners, connected Axel to a doctor who worked on getting him a state-of-the-art prosthetic at no cost to Axel and his family. Mr. Calleros affirmed that after telling his story to the class, Axel had no disciplinary incidents in high school because the teasing about his prosthetic leg stopped. As of 2021–2022, Axel did extremely well academically, passing nearly all his classes with at least a B. He made up work in summer school with high grades. Axel is succeeding and appears to be in good spirits.

Understanding and meeting the needs of a diverse student population is made more complicated by size. AUHSD schools are mid-size to large compared to other secondary schools in California. The comprehensive high schools range in size from 1,600 to 2,800 students. The junior high schools range from just under 700 to over 1,300. Educators such as Assistant Principal Calleros are eager to know about and help students with a wide range of experiences and educational needs. The puzzle is complicated and shifts over time as demographics change.

Abby and Axel are examples of extreme challenge, developing resilience, and remarkable perseverance. They may be outliers in terms of their success under adversity, but as homeless and immigrant students in poverty, their backstories are common in the district.

Figure 3.1 shows district distributions of students who were English language learners, low income, or homeless in 2021–2022.[3]

Students with low-income status are the most evenly distributed across the district. But students with background characteristics similar to Abby's and Axel's appear in different proportions in different schools. The challenge for teachers, schools, and the district as a whole is addressing the varied needs of students as they show up in different concentrations in classrooms. Figure 3.2 shows the eight schools with the highest concentrations of English language learners.

Teachers in the schools listed in figure 3.2 will have greater proportions of students advanced in and transitioning out of AUHSD's multilingual programs and thus need to be mindful of their particular learning needs. Figures 3.3 and 3.4 show that some of these same schools plus new ones have similar proportional challenges for low-income students and homeless students.

Knowing every student by name and story is a challenge that plays out differently in various schools. Gilbert High School and Magnolia High School have disproportionate numbers of students in all three groups we have named, while Western High School is disproportionate with respect to low-

FIGURE 3.1 *Prominent student groups in AUHSD, 2021–2022*

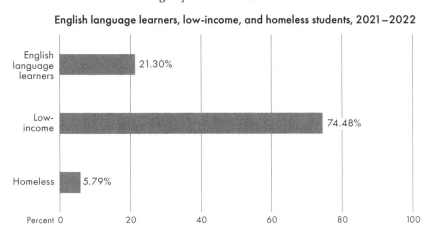

FIGURE 3.2 *Schools with proportions of English language learners greater than the district as a whole*

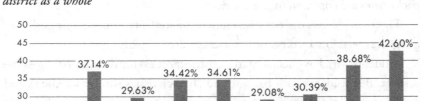

income and homeless students. These three schools provide the greatest test for AUHSD to achieve CPSF goals in ways that foster equity. As a start, for every teacher and staff member to know every student by name and story at Gilbert, Magnolia, and Western requires the educators in these schools to be able to grasp and respond positively to affective and cognitive needs that range

FIGURE 3.3 *Schools with proportions of low-income students greater than the district as a whole*

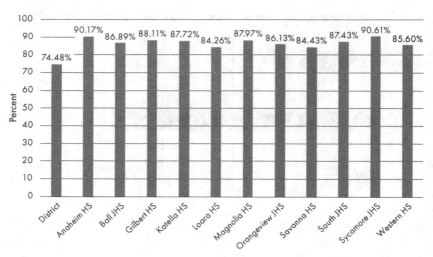

FIGURE 3.4 *Schools with proportions of homeless students greater than the district as a whole*

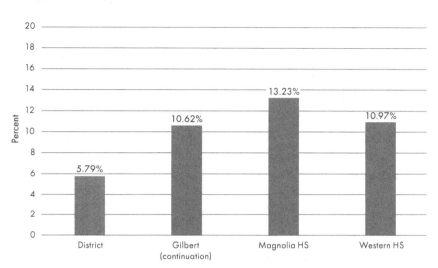

from multilingual students like Axel to war, violence, and economic refugees to students living with housing and food insecurity to students for whom home is a shelter or possibly the streets.

Adapting to Students' Needs

All the challenges named exist in all the schools, but to different degrees. The CPSF is explicitly designed to address the affective, cognitive, and dispositional needs of students who are likely to find themselves marginalized in the economy, the community, and society, without critical teaching methods, resources, and programs that reach out to them to change their life trajectories. Moving all schools toward the vital and ambitious goals of the CPSF requires understanding the nuances in student populations and providing flexible support as needed. Approaches that are either too standardized or too amorphous are likely to fail in their attempts to have students graduate from high school with a sense of purpose and the capacity to pursue it. A one-size-fits-all solution in practice results in making school better for the majority population that has always been well served. An approach in which every school does what it wants tends to provide excuses for why the kinds of students who are recent immigrants, low income, homeless, or a combination of these cannot succeed in advanced programs.[4]

Adhering to a leadership model that allows autonomy and choice to foster innovation requires school leadership to take responsibility for understanding and meeting the range of student needs as they appear in schools. If the district is to be adept at three-level chess in a way that benefits students, then principals must be able to communicate their needs to a district office that can provide resources and support to schools in different and equitable ways. The schools with the highest proportions of low-income students will likely need resources at a level and with characteristics different from the schools serving the greatest numbers of multilingual learners. Ideally, what schools design is on target for their populations, and the DO provides the personnel and resources to bring those designs to life.

> *Food for Thought 3.1*
>
> What proportion of your student population is insecure either for food, housing, or both? How is your district able to adapt to these students' needs when they attend school?

STUDENT IDENTITY CHARACTERISTICS

Too often educators assume that certain student characteristics and identities are found in tandem. For example, one might assume that the district's students of color are more likely to be in poverty. Such assumptions are not helpful in a district such as AUHSD where just about three-quarters of the students are low income. Even though a similar proportion are Hispanic or Latino, we should not assume that all or even most are English language learners. We wish to be explicit and specific about some of the important demographic highlights for the 2021–2022 academic year. Readers who want more detail about demographics within schools and across the district may wish to consult Data Quest, California's data warehouse for schools and districts.[5]

The predominant ethnic category in AUHSD is Hispanic or Latino at nearly 70 percent. Comparing this statistic to the proportion of English language learners (21.30 percent), a clear majority of Hispanic or Latino students have been living in the United States for an extended period of time, multiple generations in many cases. The next largest ethnic group is Asian, at approximately 13 percent. In California, Filipino students are counted separately from Asians and make up 4 percent of the student population. Both groups likely contain sizable proportions of recent immigrants. White students constitute 8 percent of the student body, and African Americans are less than 2 percent. Figure 3.5 shows these data graphically.

Students attend most of the district's schools in proportion to their ethnic identities. Exceptions include the schools on the wealthier side of the district and the magnet program, which tend to be whiter and more Asian than the rest of the schools. Asian students are the most overrepresented of any group, making up more than 30 percent of the population at one high school and one junior high school, and 64 percent of the population of the magnet school. The "white" descriptor masks the fact that most students in this category have Middle Eastern heritage, suggesting that the white category includes many immigrant, multilingual students of different ethnicities, including Arab and non-Arab.

Two remaining identifiers have received little or no attention up to this point. The district has a small number of foster youth attending its schools, constituting less than one-half of 1 percent of the student body. Students with disabilities make up a substantial proportion of the district's student body, at nearly 14 percent. This percentage does not include students on 504 plans or

FIGURE 3.5 *AUHSD ethnic proportions*

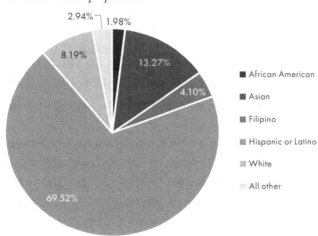

other arrangements short of qualification for special education. The proportion of students with special needs is likely quite a bit higher.

We will use these demographic data as we discuss programs, professional development, and other issues in subsequent chapters. It helps the reader to understand which students are experiencing the aspirations articulated in the CPSF, to what extent, and in what ways.

> *Food for Thought 3.2*
> What do the ethnic, racial, socioeconomic, linguistic, and disability identifiers in your school district tell you about your students' needs? What do they mask?

INDIVIDUAL MOTIVATION AND COMMUNITY MEMBERSHIP

The ideas in the heading of this section are the fundamental needs for a student population dominated by poverty with substantial doses of displacement and trauma. Students often attend secondary school having moved households more than once, lived through parental separations and family blending, and experienced school frustration and failure. Individual motivation is a necessary condition for students to take advantage of high-quality curricula and programs and engage in the world of work beyond high school. We look to two psychologists, Maslow and Herzberg, to highlight key factors teachers might consider to improve students' motivation so they are ready and eager to learn.

Many newly minted college graduates who entered education were introduced to Maslow's hierarchy of human needs, but the details are likely to escape them.[6] The familiar pyramid graphic we reproduce as figure 3.6 is ubiquitous on the internet.

With a three-fourths majority of the AUHSD student population being low income and a substantial proportion of homeless students—over 13 percent at Magnolia High School—we can confidently claim that a majority of students are seeking to meet their physiological needs of food, clothing, and shelter while striving to keep themselves safe physically and emotionally. Determining what other identifiers indicate about where students are likely

FIGURE 3.6 *Maslow's hierarchy of needs*

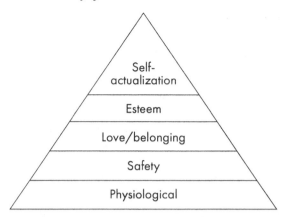

to be on Maslow's hierarchy is much more difficult. We cannot assume that all English language learners, for example, are in poverty, or that all students with disabilities have experienced persistent frustration in school. This is why knowing every student by name and story is vital to adapting to their needs in appropriate and productive ways. The school system has an imperative to elevate students at least to the level of love and belonging if they ever want to see achievement that warrants esteem (the high regard of others for work well done) or self-actualization (pursuing a purposeful life).

Motivating students to apply themselves in school and take advantage of real-world work opportunities is not as simple as feeding them, keeping schools safe, and expressing love, however. Herzberg provides the insight that there are important factors that inhibit motivation. He called these "hygiene factors," or the influences in people's lives that prevent them from focusing on work.[7] For students, these are numerous, from elevated hormones to elevated hunger, from emotional stress caused by family circumstances to embarrassment caused by peer interactions, and so on. Herzberg demonstrated in his classic research that no amount of effort to motivate workers to perform at a higher level would be effective unless and until hygiene factors were substantially improved. In schools and classrooms, this means mitigating the stressors students bring so that they can be attentive to and motivated by peers' and educators' expressions of love and belonging, praise (esteem), and opportunities for academic and workplace self-actualization.

Improving hygiene factors to activate positive motivation is not a simple task. It is possible, however, to make schools more accepting and more nurturing than they might otherwise be.

One student's self-actualization story:

In the summer of 2019, Cindy, a Latinx Anaheim High School rising senior, interned at a major local hospital. Born in Anaheim to parents from Zacatecas, Mexico, Cindy often worked with her mother cleaning homes in middle-class neighborhoods. The internship was her dream opportunity because of her ambition to become a doctor. Interning in a clinical setting in the urology department gave her the opportunity to interact with doctors and nurses, most of whom were not Latinx. (She noted that most of the janitorial and service staff looked like her parents.) Although she developed a new system for disposing of needles used in the clinic and was highly praised by her supervisors, she realized she no longer wanted to be a doctor because of the limited one-on-one time doctors spend with patients. She reflected, "I am thankful for the AIME [Anaheim Innovative Mentoring Experience] experience in that I learned that clinical doctors don't really have the time to interact with patients. I respect them a lot, but I am instead interested in a career that has more human interaction."

In early 2021, Matsuda received an email from Robert Teranishi, professor of social science and comparative education at UCLA. Dr. Teranishi wrote about an AUHSD graduate, Cindy, who amazed him with a paper about her educational experiences at Anaheim High School. As an undergraduate at a highly competitive public university who felt the pangs of imposter syndrome, Cindy wrote about how her high school education focused on the 5Cs prepared her to thrive among her peers at UCLA. Dr. Teranishi said that Cindy is an exceptional student with a strong sense of self-awareness as a Latinx woman and a disposition toward inquiry and inclusiveness. Cindy explained in her paper that her high school experience in a majority Latinx student population required her to learn about other ethnic groups' experience to prepare herself for a career in diverse settings.

Classrooms as Communities

The student stories we share in this chapter are grounded in resilience and positive responses to adversity. Families and communities provide resources to children outside school—the assets children bring to school—but these are often ignored or negated by school experiences that inhibit student choice and expression. Using the 5Cs in teaching helps students develop social skills and dispositions (twenty-first-century skills), and they are more likely to be learned by students in a supportive social system that welcomes them and aligns with their life experiences and values. We envision the classroom as a setting in which the teacher learns about her students as individuals and comes to know students collectively period by period in pursuit of a community in every classroom. By doing so, teachers apply a social systems lens to their teaching.

Building a sense of community in the classroom for many adolescents requires shifting mind-sets from defensiveness and aggression to self-confidence and cooperation. Stated differently, to be able to embed the 5Cs in teaching, students cannot be preoccupied with the hygiene factors that inhibit their motivation. Getting to such a point is tricky because teachers have limited time and resources and cannot fix what happens to students outside school. What they can do, however, is focus students' attention and make their classrooms psychologically and emotionally safe by making the assets students bring valuable in the learning process and eliminating stressful negative student-to-student interactions. Community is possible when students believe their contributions are important and everyone will be treated with respect and esteem.

Community in the classroom occurs when students are free to express themselves genuinely—raise their voices—while being open to and accepted by others with similar and different perspectives. When students' opinions and contributions are seen as inherently valuable, school is motivating and self-actualizing rather than anxiety-producing or demeaning. This sense of community can be established through application of Collaboration and Compassion as classroom routines that generate positive and productive habits of mind.

> *Food for Thought 3.3*
> Why do some students in your schools feel a strong sense of belonging while others do not? What does community in the classroom look like? How might that affect the school as a community?

SCOPING THE WORLD OF WORK

Adapting to students' affective needs such as their motivation and a sense of belonging to a community help to build twenty-first-century skills, but schools and districts must also shape learning experiences so that students, given their identities and prior experiences, will be able to find their place in the world of work after high school. There are multiple pathways students might follow, from part-time community college attendance while working full-time to full-time devotion to a four-year college education. There are two common threads among graduates' possible experiences that lead to purposeful life: (1) students will need some kind of post–high school education to move into a lifelong career, and (2) what that career will look like cannot be entirely known at present. Consequently, students will need the kinds of skills, knowledge, and dispositions that will allow them to adapt to changing work environments. We have some clues about what this means.

Nearly half of all jobs are likely to be eliminated by technology in the next twenty years.[8] Furthermore, the employability gap between the skills employers need and the skills workers have is growing larger. Skills range from the soft skills embedded in the 5Cs to understanding basic mathematics to communicating clearly in writing. Most school systems are not yet addressing the distance between what students know and are able to do upon high school graduation and what employers are seeking.[9] Economists project that thousands of well-paying jobs that exist today will disappear, unlikely ever to return. The main cause for the changing job landscape is not outsourcing, but automation technology that makes producing goods and services more efficient. As jobs disappear and careers morph, new jobs will require workers to obtain new skills and knowledge sets to fill yet unknown roles.

Schools and districts need to focus their attention on how to educate students today for midcareer employability when the class of 2023 turns thirty-five in 2040. No one can foretell the future, which is why the CPSF focuses attention on educating the whole student. The belief in AUHSD is that affective and cognitive strength, coupled with self-awareness, self-esteem, and a clear sense of purpose, prepares graduates to adapt to work and career changes we cannot now predict with any degree of certainty. Clearer is the fact that the currently dominant model of secondary education doesn't build on the strengths of and adapt to the needs of students who make up the majority of the AUHSD population. Fundamental change is needed if schools are to make a difference in students' social and economic mobility.

> **Food for Thought 3.4**
> What needs in your local economy are not being met? How might graduates from your schools fit in? Do graduates know what opportunities are available to them?

THE LOGIC OF THE CPSF

The student population in AUHSD is predominantly low income and nonwhite and therefore in need of educational experiences that move beyond a suburban model dominated by college preparation. Furthermore, large proportions of students face life circumstances that tighten the shackles of poverty, such as the need to learn English, homelessness, and, as in all school districts, learning disabilities. The district recognizes that these students face life challenges and at the same time have personal assets that are typically underappreciated and ignored in public school systems.

Figure 3.7 presents a reminder of how AUHSD perceives the interconnectedness among cognition, affect, and student success. Technical skills are essential. To be successful in any aspect of the economy and society requires literacy, the capacity to calculate and analyze quantitative data, and the ability to connect humanities, the arts, and science to understand and address the world's problems. Technical skills are about more than preparing for college; they are the skills necessary for work and personal progress. Many students, especially the population in AUHSD, are unable to accelerate their acquisition of technical skills because they haven't developed their ability to learn from others through collaboration, thinking critically, engaging in creative problem-solving, or communicating what they are thinking. These twenty-first-century skills are essential complements to technical skills because they give students the ability to process information, connections, and outcomes that are not self-evident, particularly to this student population. The twenty-first-century skills we have named are four of the 5Cs. The fifth—compassion—is the anchor for building positive relationships and participating in civic engagement.

The interaction between technical skills and twenty-first-century skills creates the possibility of elevating youth voice and purpose, particularly for a

FIGURE 3.7 *Career Preparedness Systems Framework (CPSF)*

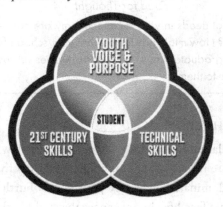

student population that has typically been silenced and marginalized. As our examples of Anjelica and Anthony in chapter 1 demonstrated, not all students know their purpose by the time they graduate, but they can develop a clear sense of where they want to go next when given the right educational experiences and supports.

> *Food for Thought 3.5*
> How are twenty-first-century skills taught in your schools? Is this teaching tailored to students' identities, life experiences, assets, and needs?

SCHOOLS WORKING FOR STUDENTS

The CPSF is a theory of action that claims that technical skills and twenty-first-century skills, when carefully developed, will help more students graduate from high school with a life plan and the capacity to pursue it. It is up to the educators in AUHSD, those in interested school districts, and researchers to demonstrate the validity or fallacy of this theory of action in contexts of highly challenged students.

We encourage teachers, board members, parents, and community members to give careful consideration to their student populations to assess what they need to live fulfilling, gratifying lives. Priorities will differ by district context. One district's students may need closer connection to a particular culture. In another, curriculum and pedagogy may be misaligned with the student population, being either too remote or not challenging enough. Yet another district may find that students' life circumstances keep them isolated from the world outside their neighborhoods. In numerous urban and inner-ring suburban districts, all three priorities and more will be at the forefront. Educators may see their own student populations in the AUHSD profile, suggesting they might emulate many of AUHSD's approaches. Others will find meaningful differences in their own student populations and use different tactics. Most readers will likely find some similarities and differences.

Chapter 4 describes signature programs endemic to the CPSF and how they were designed with an understanding of who the students are and how they intend to elevate youth voice and purpose. We provide evidence of program success—who is being reached and who may still be missing out. Further, we aspire to show readers how these programs were built so that they may take lessons learned into their own schools and districts. We would not expect other school districts to replicate all of the programs in AUHSD. What we hope is that readers will see how programs, curricula, professional relationships, professional development, and systems thinking, human relations, organizational learning, and instructional leadership work together to educate all students for purposeful life.

> **TAKING STOCK**
>
> Sometimes when we dig into district demographic data, we find surprises. In AUHSD, the number of homeless students was a real eye-opener, not only because of the numbers but because seeing the numbers made us stop and think more carefully about how much more difficult school is when you do not have a consistent, dry, warm place to lay your head. We encourage you to look carefully at your district's demographics and how that varies across schools to figure out the most prevalent assets and needs and how they are distributed. The following questions may spur your thinking:
>
> 1. Which portion of the student population is most engaged in the best that the district has to offer? Why them?
> 2. Which portion of the student population seems to be missing out on the best that the district has to offer? Why them?
> 3. For the students who appear to be missing out, in what ways might schools and classrooms adapt themselves so that these students might find themselves in an empowering community?

CHAPTER 4

BUILDING A NETWORK TO ELEVATE YOUTH VOICE AND PURPOSE

> Artificial intelligence has just been something that I've always kind of heard about since I've always been interested in computer science and things like that. Last year, we had [a guest speaker] who was talking about AI and I think that was the first time I heard about it in a more academic setting. Before the senior year registration, [high school principal] Dr. Hernandez reached out to me . . . about this internship opportunity. I took it because it sounded amazing.
>
> —ALAYSIA, JOHN F. KENNEDY HIGH SCHOOL GRADUATE

HIGH SCHOOL STUDENTS working in artificial intelligence (AI) internships? Learning about AI from an expert and then taking advantage of an opportunity to work in a technology company that uses AI is an example of the ideal CPSF experience. Although career and technical education (CTE) has been a part of secondary school education in the United States for well over a hundred years, connecting a career pathway discovered in high school classrooms to actual part-time work in the career field is highly unusual. That Alaysia as a mixed-race (Black and Latina) young woman has leveraged her internship experience to pursue a computer science degree is revolutionary, given that people like her made up less than 5 percent of the computer-related workforce in 2020.[1]

NEW PROCESSES SUSTAIN AND IMPROVE THE FUNDAMENTALS

An education revolution that inspires young women like Alaysia and students from all underrepresented identities is exactly what is needed to expand their worldview and aspirations beyond the difficult circumstances in which they have grown up. Motivation coupled to the skills and knowledge to achieve gratifying work will enrich their adulthood. Yet, it is often hard to see the need for changes in the test-oriented status quo. Rachel Carson, pioneer of the environmental movement, famously said,

> *The road we have long been traveling is deceptively easy, a smooth superhighway on which we progress with great speed, but at its end lies disaster. The other fork of the road—the one less traveled by—offers our last, our only chance to reach a destination that assures the preservation of the earth* [emphasis added].[2]

The quotation from her 1962 landmark book, *Silent Spring*, is as timely a warning about the environment as it is about education, because we depend on the generation now in school to solve problems not of their own making. As of this writing, many of the dire consequences from thoughtless exploitation of Earth that Carson and other scientists predicted have come true. Wars, famine, drought, floods, and fires are the new normal that our children must face and somehow be prepared for. The cities, suburbs, and rural areas where K–12 students live are all impacted. They make up a world that can be confusing and induce anxiety for students whom we are counting on to create effective solutions for puzzles that today appear unsolvable.

Educators and their communities have a moral imperative to prepare students for the local, state, national, and global circumstances shaped by previous generations. Empowering students to see their communities' challenges with clarity and do meaningful work requires all of them to have access to the great benefits and opportunities their schools can make available. Students must learn the skills and knowledge that help address the kinds of pathologies Rachel Carson imagined.

Educators need new drivers toward improved educational experiences that will transform schools and systems to position students as problem-solvers who can lift themselves up and by doing so improve their communities and the country at large. Focusing more on *classroom processes* that generate test scores and other outcomes and less on the test scores themselves is the best way to learn how to help students take advantage of school programs and community resources while overcoming constraints and bias that limit opportunity.

Fullan and Quinn, in *Coherence, the Right Drivers for Schools, Districts and Systems*, suggest that it is better to strive for high school graduates ready to succeed instead of maintaining a narrow focus on college and career readiness.[3] These authors argue that education systems have squandered time and resources on the wrong drivers. We interpret life readiness to be students' ability upon graduation to pursue their life goals as nurtured and developed through their secondary school education experiences. The implications are that students must have cognitive skills, affective skills, and inspiration to define their own purpose, pursue it successfully, and assume a productive and gratifying place in the community, economy, and society. Fullan and Quinn point to six Cs, what they refer to as the new global competencies: character, citizenship, collaboration, communication, creativity, and critical thinking.[4]

Fullan and Quinn's six Cs closely align with AUHSD's 5Cs—Collaboration, Communication, Creativity, Critical Thinking, and Compassion. In AUHSD, Fullan's citizenship "c" is embedded in the AUHSD vision that references graduates as "civic-minded." Schools, the district, for-profit, nonprofit, and governmental systems are woven together interdependently to provide opportunities for students to engage as committed citizens in their schools, the workplace, and the community.

From Test Scores to College Degrees

Helping students look outward toward their futures helps AUHSD avoid being driven by standardized tests and mindless "teaching to the test." For seven years, the district has eliminated benchmark assessments or interim assessments and never prioritized test scores in teacher evaluation. Instead, striving for improved student motivation, sound content teaching, demonstrated relevance, and opportunities for meaningful work have yielded noticeable growth in the district's Smarter Balanced Assessment Consortium (SBAC) English language arts (ELA) test scores as students move from eighth grade to eleventh grade (see figure 4.1).[5] For example, the eighth-grade cohort tested in 2018 improved their overall proficiency rate by nearly 20 percentage points in ELA when they were tested in eleventh grade in 2021. The same cohort improved math proficiency by four percentage points (see figure 4.2). Test score declines resulting from pandemic disruptions were modest compared to other California districts, and the district continues to outperform the State of California in the economically disadvantaged category. In 2022, 35 percent of low-income students statewide met or exceeded standards in ELA.[6] In

FIGURE 4.1 *Percentage of students meeting and exceeding standards in English language arts on SBAC assessments*

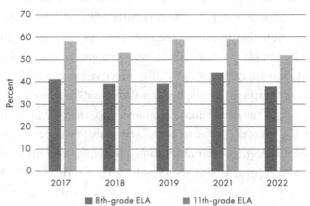

AUHSD, where nearly 75 percent of students are low income, 52 percent of all students met or exceeded standards in ELA in 2022.

The district is not complacent about achievement levels, but results are encouraging. Remembering that AUHSD does not educate these cohorts of students until they reach seventh grade, it is clear from figures 4.1 and 4.2 that as students spend longer periods of time in the system, their performance improves noticeably when nationwide proficiency levels tend to drop in later grades.[7] What these figures also reveal is that high school achievement as indicated by these specific metrics has remained steady or rising for four of the past five years, while post-COVID achievement in 2022 declined less than ten percentage points and was approximately 5 percent higher than the statewide average for California. Compared to low-income students in California, AUHSD's student population scored seventeen percentage points higher in ELA and nearly the same as the state as a whole in math.[8] These test score comparisons are one high-level indicator that CPSF strategies are as or more effective for low-income students as test-focused schooling in which subgroups of students tend to be marginalized.

The effects of shifting focus away from test scores and toward learning that matters to students are apparent beyond high school graduation. AUHSD graduates have demonstrated high performance and persistence at the University of California, Irvine (UCI), and California State University, Fuller-

FIGURE 4.2 *Percentage of students meeting and exceeding standards in mathematics on SBAC assessments*

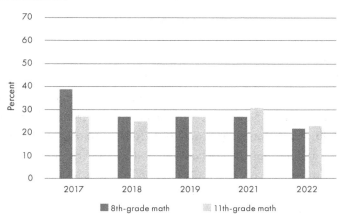

ton (CSUF), AUHSD's closest four-year universities. Low-income AUHSD students in these local four-year universities have outperformed their higher-income peers from other school districts. Table 4.1 displays results from UCI that report AUHSD students with strong college GPAs and persistence rates higher than four-year students at UCI and nationally.

Table 4.1 demonstrates the power of dual-enrollment opportunities in AUHSD and the quality of college preparation. Note that the seventy members of the class of 2021 attending UCI had earned an average of thirty-four units in their first college semester. A typical course load would be fifteen units, meaning that these students matriculated with a substantial amount of dual-enrollment units. A typical BA at UCI requires 120 units, with some

TABLE 4.1 *AUHSD graduates attending University of California, Irvine*

AUHSD graduating class	Total enrolled at UCI	Average units earned	Average GPA	AUHSD retention rate
2018	141	171	3.41	95%
2019	147	122	3.44	95%
2020	122	77	3.40	99%
2021	70	34	N/A	N/A

majors requiring more. The AUHSD class of 2018 graduated from the university with far more than 120 units by 2022. AUHSD students continue at UCI each year at a rate that far exceeds the national average of 62 to 68 percent.[9] Their average GPA indicates high performance and high potential to pursue graduate degrees.

College admissions data provided by CSUF demonstrate the level of success AUHSD students experience being admitted to and beginning a four-year college path. Figure 4.3 displays the percentage of AUHSD students admitted to CSUF for four graduating classes. The admission rate generally climbs for the district and for individual schools until 2021, the first graduating class to experience more than a year of COVID-19 effects on education and families.

We can see from figure 4.3 that most of the district's high schools cluster close to the average rate of admission, while Cypress and Kennedy stand out as generally above average. These two high schools are also well below the district's percentage of low-income students that hovers close to 75 percent. Anaheim High School's proportion of low-income students is 20 percent higher than the district as a whole, and its admission rate is below the district average.[10] This connection between the proportion of low-income students and admission to CSUF generally holds across the district's high schools, though it is not as pronounced as with the three schools named.

FIGURE 4.3 *AUHSD and individual high school percent of applicants admitted to California State University, Fullerton*

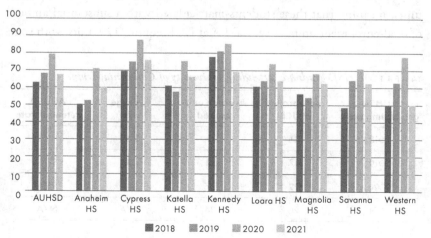

The percent of admitted students enrolling in CSUF is shown in figure 4.4. The data pattern shifts dramatically with the lowest-income high school, Anaheim, having some of the highest percentages of admitted students enrolled. Cypress's percentages are substantially below the district average, while Kennedy's percentage is above in 2018 and 2019 and below in 2020 and 2021.

Enrollment rates are somewhat difficult to interpret because of the range of reasons for deciding to enroll elsewhere, from financial decisions to attend community college at substantially lower cost to admission into a more selective university. What is clear from the data is that, for most AUHSD schools, between 30 and 50 percent of admitted graduates choose to enroll at CSUF.

CSUF provided data that allow us to compare AUHSD graduates to those from other school districts admitted to and enrolling in CSUF.[11] Figure 4.5 shows that AUHSD graduates are admitted at higher rates than the average of all other school districts' applicants to CSUF.

Similarly, figure 4.6 shows that AUHSD admitted students enroll at higher rates compared to students coming from other school districts. The admissions and enrollment data taken together demonstrate a higher propensity for AUHSD graduates to succeed at CSUF compared to their peers from other districts.

UCI's deputy director at the Center for Educational Partnerships, Santana Ruiz, summarizes what he believes to be the factors that distinguish AUHSD graduates for college admission and success:

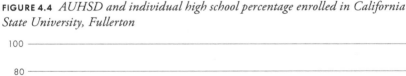

FIGURE 4.4 *AUHSD and individual high school percentage enrolled in California State University, Fullerton*

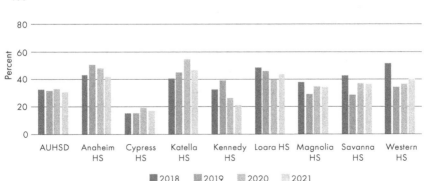

FIGURE 4.5 *AUHSD admission rates to California State University, Fullerton, compared to all other applicants*

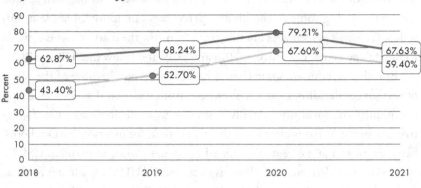

AUHSD cohort success is due to three factors: (1) that graduates enter the university with a sense of purpose and voice, (2) AUHSD leads Orange County with students having significant units in dual credit, and (3) the 5Cs give students a better grounding in emotional intelligence that helps them pivot more effectively in response to life's challenges.[12]

The three factors highlighted by Ruiz mirror the foundational categories of the CPSF—student voice, technical skills, and twenty-first-century skills. This chapter details specific AUHSD programs in depth, explaining their

FIGURE 4.6 *AUHSD enrollment rates to California State University, Fullerton, compared to all other applicants*

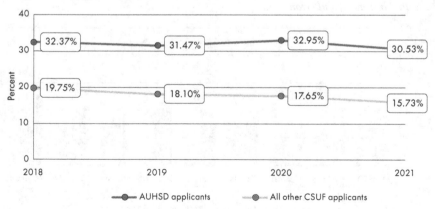

linkages to student voice and purpose and life beyond high school. We place special emphasis on two broad areas: (1) demonstrating program effectiveness with data; and (2) explaining how these programs were put into place. AUHSD is achieving unprecedented outcomes for students with an approach that integrates multiple school and nonschool systems through specific implementation actions within a learning organization culture of collaboration, accountability, and coherence.

> *Food for Thought 4.1*
> How are twenty-first-century skills taught in your schools? Is this teaching tailored to students' identities, life experiences, assets, and needs?

PARTNERSHIPS IN SUPPORT OF STUDENTS

Building relationships between K–12 school districts and higher education institutions can be difficult. The success that AUHSD graduates have enjoyed and recognition from one university's office of educational partnerships is due in large measure to the formation of the Anaheim Educational Collaborative. This is a unique consortium consisting of three clusters of constituents: (1) K–12 institutions including AUHSD, the Anaheim Elementary School District, the North Orange County Regional Occupational Program, and the Orange County Office of Education; (2) the two local community colleges, Cypress College and Fullerton College; California State University, Fullerton; and the University of California, Irvine; and (3) civic organizations that include the City of Anaheim, the United Way, and the TGR Foundation (Tiger Woods's philanthropy). In 2017, all members of this partnership committed to the Anaheim Educational Pledge.[13] This groundbreaking promise to all students and families served by all the named entities specifically supports AUHSD's emphasis on the 5Cs, the expansion of dual enrollment, and greater emphasis on career and life readiness. The pledge carries the imprimatur of the school district superintendents, the chancellors of the four-year universities, and the chancellor of the North Orange County Community College district that includes Cypress and Fullerton colleges, and the mayor of the City of Anaheim.

One of the significant outcomes of the Anaheim Educational Collaborative and the Anaheim Educational Pledge is the expansion of dual-enrollment opportunities. An important means of helping low-income, immigrant students pursue post–high school education is to provide opportunities to earn college credit and high school credit simultaneously. When families are struggling with parents working multiple jobs just to pay rent and put food on the table, it is hard for them to imagine forgoing family income so that high school graduate family members can attend college. Often the need for family income interferes with high school education as well. By helping students accelerate their high school and college progress while still students legally compelled to attend school, AUHSD is able to support families as their children invest in higher education. College credits earned in high school reduce tuition and supplies costs incurred in college and shorten the time to a certificate, degree, or transfer to a four-year university. Dual enrollment plays a critical role in students finding and pursuing their life purpose.

AUHSD leads Orange County with over 1,100 students enrolled in one or more dual-enrollment courses in 2022. Figure 4.7 displays districtwide comprehensive high school participation in dual enrollment and the percentage

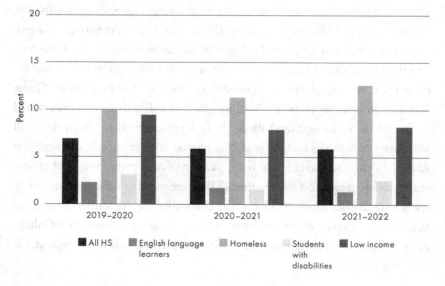

FIGURE 4.7 *Dual enrollment in courses earning high school and community college credit simultaneously*

of students from four subgroups relative to their numbers in the total student population. For example, 10 percent of the homeless student population was enrolled in one or more dual-enrollment courses in 2019–2020.

Dual enrollment for all district students has held steady over the three academic years 2019–2020 to 2021–2022, hovering between 6 and 7 percent of the total AUHSD population, even during the worst pandemic year of 2020–2021. Participation rates for English language learners and students with disabilities have declined somewhat, while low-income students and students classified as homeless participated in dual enrollment in proportions substantially larger than the population as a whole. The participation rate of homeless students grew over the three years.

The current capacity of the dual-enrollment program fostered by the Anaheim Educational Pledge is one of the district's equity drivers as low-income and homeless students find a feasible pathway to higher education. AUHSD, with its nearly 70 percent Hispanic or Latino population, bucks California statewide trends in which Black and Latino students are underrepresented in dual-enrollment programs.[14] Dual enrollment is recognized by higher education leaders as one of the many features of education in AUHSD that supports a higher success rate at local two-year colleges and four-year universities.

Development of Dual Enrollment

The Anaheim Educational Collaborative and the Anaheim Educational Pledge established commitment and accountability across institutions. Coherence required aligning the teacher association and AUHSD administration so that educators within AUHSD would help bring dual enrollment to fruition. Coherence did not come easily. Dr. Jaron Fried, assistant superintendent of instruction, met with then Anaheim Secondary Teachers Association (ASTA) president Dean Elder to explore the concept in 2017. Elder was approaching the last year of his presidency. Although an instructional leader at heart and a supporter of Matsuda as he became superintendent, Elder did not want to concede to anything that reeked of selling out to the district. The teacher association could not be in the position of standing idly by while class sections and teaching position full-time equivalents (FTE) were transferred to community college instructors teaching courses in which students could earn both high school and college credit. Fried reminded Elder that dual enrollment was good for students as it gave them more options in accumulating college credits. Fried explained that dual enrollment would not impact union membership because high school teaching sections would not be lost. Instead, Fried promised not to seek cost savings through personnel reductions. Dual enrollment would actually benefit students and teachers in standard high school classes by reducing class size. For example, a senior English class taught by a college professor would free up a high school teacher to teach a different section in a course impacted with high enrollment, thus spreading the same number of students over more class sections. Elder, generally trusting Fried and the district administration, agreed and supported piloting dual enrollment. Agreement with ASTA opened the door to instruction in cutting-edge career pathways such as cybersecurity, AI, drone technology, biotechnology, and entrepreneurship, as well as engaging courses such as ethnic studies.

In chapter 2 we referenced another potential stumbling block with dual-enrollment courses—textbook adoption—when discussing the trim tab concept. AUHSD recognizes that institutions at different levels with different roles within the community sometimes have interests that clash. The Anaheim Educational Collaborative as a deliberative body and the Anaheim Educational Pledge as a public commitment provide the glue that holds the process of working out differences together. Their examination of district data and collaborative solution finding are examples of organizational learning that takes place at level three. Early success within the collaborative motivates the numerous and varied stakeholders to continue their support of these vital partnerships.

CTE in AUHSD

[T]he most urgent social issue affecting poor people and people of color is economic access.

—BOB MOSES, FOUNDER, THE ALGEBRA PROJECT[15]

At the dawn of career education in public high schools in the early twentieth century, vocational education was intended for "hand-minded" students who were not likely to succeed in an academic curriculum. Vocational education was seen as an opportunity for low-income, immigrant students to find a place in the economy and society.[16] Unfortunately for students interested in entering the workforce without attending four-year college, vocational education struggled to change with the times, and vocational courses acquired the stigma that they were intended only for low-achieving students.

It is easy to forget that vocational education was a Progressive reform intended to expand opportunities for the immigrant or agrarian poor. It is in the spirit of creating opportunities that the descendant of vocational education, CTE, strives to help students discover fulfilling work prospects and the relevance of high school and college coursework. The CPSF embraces CTE as an important means for students to discover their purpose as contributors to the community and the local economy and future breadwinners for their families. There are three essential distinctions between CTE education in AUHSD today and the vocational education that prevailed in the twentieth century: (1) CTE pathways, rather than one-off courses, are present in every school, (2) CTE courses reflect the contemporary economy and the need for highly educated workers in various fields, and (3) CTE moves beyond the secondary school classroom into dual-enrollment courses and internships that are pathway-aligned.[17]

The district's high schools all support career pathways. Some pathways focus on more traditional careers that are unlikely to be replaced by automation, such as public safety. Others represent cutting-edge fields. Table 4.2 presents the complete district offering.

CTE pathways in AUSHD help generate equity in two ways: (1) a wide range of offerings at all the schools ensures choice for students across the spectrum of identities and post–high school interests, and (2) the policy that allows students to take courses in a pathway other than those found at their home school avoids the problem of students missing out based on residence. CTE participation data reported to the California Department of Education reveal AUHSD's progress on this aspect of the CPSF. The state uses broader categories than the course titles in table 4.2, but they reveal districtwide results. A CTE "participant" is any student who has taken one or more courses in a state-approved CTE pathway. A "completer" for state reporting purposes has completed a two-course sequence with passing grades. Figure 4.8 shows districtwide participation rates in CTE pathways broken out by the student identifiers that California uses in this reporting. The percentages for student subgroups are based on their overall presence in the district. For example, there were 2,486 high school students with disabilities enrolled in the district

TABLE 4.2 *Career and technical education pathways available at each AUHSD high school*

Anaheim	Cypress	Katella	Kennedy
Biotechnology	Law and justice	Film and Digital Arts Academy	Artificial intelligence
Child development	Child development	Child development	Design, visual, and media arts
Design, visual, and media arts	Design, visual, and media arts	Engineering design	Education
Entrepreneurship and self-employment	Engineering design	Food service and hospitality	Entrepreneurship and self-employment
Food service and hospitality	Entrepreneurship and self-employment	Patient care	Finance services, accounting, and banking
Patient care— Dental	Food service and hospitality	Public safety— JROTC	Food service and hospitality
Production and managerial arts	Games and simulations	Software and systems development	Patient care
Public Safety Academy	Patient care	System diagnostics and services	Production and managerial arts
Public safety— JROTC	Production and managerial arts		Public safety— JROTC
Residential and commercial construction	Software and systems development		
Software and systems development			

Loara	Magnolia	Savanna	Western
Drone technology	Magnolia Cybersecurity Institute	Savanna Medical Careers Academy	AUHSD Incubator Lab (iLab)
Child development	Education	Food service and hospitality	Creators for Change Academy
Design, visual, and media arts	Patient care	Production and managerial arts	Design, visual, and media arts
Finance services, accounting, and banking	Production and managerial arts	Residential and commercial construction	Food service and hospitality
Patient care— Sports medicine	Public safety— JROTC	System diagnostics and services	Patient care— Community health-care worker

Loara	Magnolia	Savanna	Western
Production and managerial arts	*Public safety— Law enforcement*		*Performing arts— Dance*
Public safety— JROTC	Residential and commercial construction		Production and managerial arts
Software systems development			Public safety— JROTC
System diagnostics and services			Residential and commercial construction
			Software and systems development

Cambridge Virtual Academy	Gilbert High School	Oxford Academy	
Design, visual, and media arts	*Business Design Academy*	Biotechnology	
Entrepreneurship and self-employment	*Financial services*	Engineering design	
Software and systems development	Food service and hospitality	Entrepreneurship and self-employment	
	Patient care	Software and systems development	

Note: Pathways unique to a school are in italics.

in 2022, and 1,648 of them enrolled in one or more CTE courses, making their participation rate 66 percent.

Just over 60 percent of AUHSD students take one or more CTE pathway courses in their high schools. Students with disabilities (SWD), low-income students, and homeless students participate at a higher than the districtwide rate for all students.[18] English language learner students participate at a rate somewhat lower than the district as a whole. The language barrier for students in the first two levels of English language development likely explains this difference. Overall, equity indicators are strong as students typically excluded from innovative programs participate in CTE.

The case for equitable participation in CTE is further supported by examining individual school data. Figure 4.9 reveals that schools' total participation rates cluster near 60 percent for the district as a whole. Representation for

FIGURE 4.8 *Districtwide participation rates in Career and Technical Education pathways, by student subgroups, 2022*

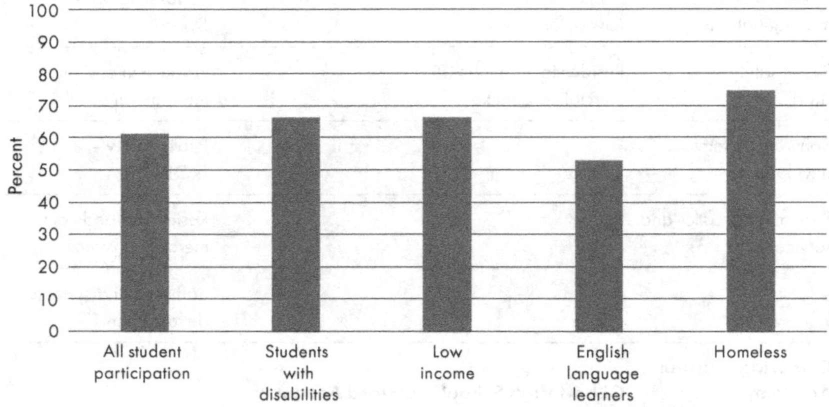

SWD, low-income students, and homeless students is generally higher than each school's total student population participation, and English language learners participate at a lower rate at all the schools. Students have access to the benefits of CTE no matter which school they happen to attend.[19]

AUHSD arrived at the newer CTE pathways, shown in table 4.2, through community partnerships, often in collaboration with the North Orange County Regional Occupation Program. Beginning with what contemporary

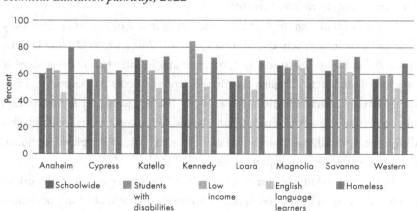

FIGURE 4.9 *Participation rates by school and student subgroups in Career and Technical Education pathways, 2022*

work looks like in the Orange County and Anaheim communities, business leaders and educators collaborated with AUHSD teachers and administrators to design courses that would teach the technical skills and soft skills needed for graduates to have meaningful and gratifying twenty-first-century jobs. CTE pathway development is a vivid example of successful three-level chess that has substantially changed CTE experiences available to AUHSD students.

Reverse-Engineering Career Pathways

The AUHSD cybersecurity pathway was developed in 2017 and was unique in that it was a partnership that crossed traditional boundaries of K–12 education, higher education, and the broader community. The design of the cybersecurity pathway included district teachers, a community college dean in business and computer science, and an Anaheim Innovative Mentoring Experience (AIME) corporate partner, MeridianLink. Dean Henry Hua of Cypress College said:

> I was proud to be part of something special, to reverse-engineer a pathway with the corporate end-user that would lead to real jobs in cybersecurity. The [community college] dual-credit courses were developed with input from MeridianLink. One seldom sees a corporate partner so involved in developing jobs.[20]

Tim Nguyen, chief strategy officer of MeridianLink, added:

> If you think about it, from a corporate and nonprofit perspective, it makes sense to integrate job requirements and skills in a K–12 system. The 5Cs and focus on student purpose are really game-changers for us in that students have real skills and aspirations for success in careers and in life. AUHSD is a forward-thinking district that operates like a learning organization and can implement new ideas that align with its vision and mission. Reverse-engineering jobs with MeridianLink and Cypress College created a template that led to other innovative pathways.[21]

Community member Nguyen is the first Vietnamese American to take a company from startup to the New York Stock Exchange. He freely lends his expertise to the district to ensure that technical coursework and twenty-first-century skills development address workplace needs. In his current role as the driving force behind an educational technology startup, Nguyen serves as an informal adviser to Matsuda and Fried's education division team. As a result, he helps to foster learning about the world of work not just for students, but for AUHSD educators. At the same time, keeping coursework focused on actual work skills and knowledge generates coherence from the classroom into internships and the world of full-time work.

CTE ON THE CUTTING EDGE: CYBERSECURITY. Magnolia High School teachers working collaboratively with the cybersecurity development partners created the Magnolia Cybersecurity Institute. Figure 4.10 is a graphic representation of the pathway that students can enter starting in seventh grade. The lower portion of the graphic shows that there are sub-specialties within the pathway that can address a variety of student interests.

Whether a cutting-edge CTE pathway is an equity driver reaching students most in need of access to such an experience is determined by student participation data. Figure 4.11 shows the overall 2021–2022 participation rate in cybersecurity courses and that of three student subgroups.

FIGURE 4.10 *Cybersecurity pathway for feeder middle schools and Magnolia High School*

FIGURE 4.11 *Student participation in all cybersecurity pathway courses, 2021–2022*

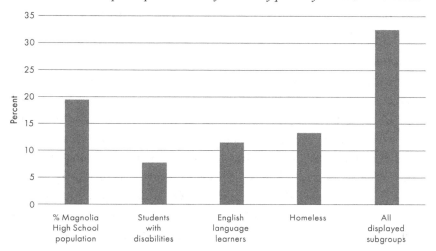

Slightly less than 20 percent (324) of all Magnolia High School students participated in one or more cybersecurity courses. SWD, English language learners, and homeless students together comprised over 30 percent of the students in cybersecurity courses, demonstrating their positively disproportionate representation in this unique opportunity to find life purpose in high technology. Another indicator of equity and opportunity comes from knowing that SWD, English language learners, and homeless students comprise over 60 percent of the Magnolia student population. Thus, approximately half of the students with these identifiers are represented in the cybersecurity pathway.[22]

Another equity dimension specific to high technology and the cybersecurity pathway is gender. Nearly 40 percent of cybersecurity participants are female, in sharp contrast to technology jobs in general, 75 percent of which are filled by males. Female AUHSD students identified the key factor that enables the district to run across the labor market grain toward equity. Their interest was spurred by a skilled, inspiring Filipina American teacher, Jamie Keledjian. A career-switcher teacher with professional experience in cybersecurity, Keledjian deliberately assumes the role of mentor because she understands firsthand the challenges young women will face as they enter the world of tech work. She is committed to young women's success.[23] Keledjian stands as a prominent example of a teacher leader capable of playing three-level chess.[24]

She understands the community (level three) and the classroom (level one) and leverages district resources (level two) to be an effective mentor for young women interested in high technology.

UNLEASHING GENIUS: THE ILAB. One of the most unusual K–12 programs the district has initiated is the region's first incubator lab, the hub for classroom-to-product ideas emanating from CTE coursework. Located at Western High School, the iLab is designed to address the immense challenge for urban, low-income students across the United States in accessing intellectual and social capital. Matsuda was inspired to address innovation through CTE by an article in the *Atlantic* about research from economist Raj Chetty. Chetty found that neighborhoods replicate themselves in profound ways. Children who grow up in the presence of adults who held patents were more likely themselves to be granted patents. The opposite was also true—students whose families were not in professional-level jobs and generating new ideas were less likely to have careers that gave them opportunities to innovate. At the same time, the phenomenon of innovative neighborhoods perpetuates income disparities when students find themselves in the "wrong neighborhood" for innovation.[25] If the school district and corporate partners could spur students to become innovators, Matsuda reasoned, then maybe Anaheim could become a more innovative hub that generates new jobs and careers. School experiences would supplement family support to break out of predetermined work and income patterns. Matsuda pushed for AUHSD to have its own incubator lab when he read Chetty's work. According to the *Atlantic* article:

> [Opportunity Insights] find that children from families in the top 1 percent of income distribution are 10 times as likely to have filed for a patent as those from below-median-income families, and that white children are three times as likely to have filed a patent as black children. This means, they say, that there could be millions of "lost Einsteins"—individuals who might have become inventors and changed the course of American life, had they grown up in different neighborhoods. "There are very large gaps in innovation by income, race, and gender," according to Chetty. "These gaps don't seem to be about differences in ability to innovate—they seem directly related to the environment.[26]

Alaysia's AIME internship with Loko.AI mentioned in the quote that opens this chapter is an illustration of how bringing innovation opportunities to students from neighborhoods without the innovation opportunities found among families with registered patents can benefit students and remake the community. The investment in Alysia via the AI pathway took her interests to higher levels. Students like her are now able to take what they learn from a particular field and explore their creativity in the iLab. Pathways, in conjunction with the iLab, help to identify potentially lost Einsteins. Alaysia's story proves the point. Her school experience coupled with her Loko.AI internship provided a unique and targeted attempt to place her ahead of competition from more privileged school districts to enter a highly competitive major and fast-paced industry. Her hard work and initiative paid off as she was accepted to Brown, Penn, Cornell, Columbia, Carnegie Mellon, Cal Poly Pomona, MIT, UCI, UCSD, and UCLA. She is currently attending MIT.

Discovering potentially lost Einsteins such as Alaysia inspired Matsuda, teachers, and partners. Particularly compelling was Chetty's assertion that "if women, minorities, and children from low- and middle-income families invented at the same rate as white men from high-income families, there would be four times as many inventors in America as there are today."[27] Matsuda reasoned that the district could create an ecosystem of innovation through the Anaheim Educational Collaborative and the AIME program, with an anchor incubator lab at centrally located Western High School.[28] The goal is to create a culture of innovation and problem-solving that can motivate students to learn how to monetize their ideas, including learning about patents that will be generated through cutting-edge pathways such as AI, biotechnology, cybersecurity, and drone technology. (See figure 4.12.)

iLab participation in 2021–2022, the first year of implementation, is robust, with 228 students enrolled in four different iLab courses. This represents a little over 13 percent of the Western High School population. Figure 4.13 shows that, similar to cybersecurity, SWD, English language learners, and homeless students participate in the program at rates as high or higher than the overall student population. Collectively, these subgroups of students represent over 50 percent of all iLab students. Potentially lost Einsteins are getting a chance to show what they can do in AUHSD.

Summary: Organizational Learning and Instructional Leadership

Working with multiple partners to identify potential pathways and career-focused programs requires a willingness to examine the challenge of career

FIGURE 4.12 *AUHSD explanation of pathway to and through the iLab*

opportunity that identifies how the status quo limits access for marginalized students. Older CTE pathways, for example, when offered alone, might relegate low-income students to low-paying jobs. AUHSD and its partners probe the status quo for change opportunities and exploit them with innovations such as the cybersecurity pathway and the iLab. To make these programs important in schools requires instructional leadership at level one that applies knowledge of levels two and three resources at the school and classroom levels. Participation data reveal evidence of a changed status quo and instructional leadership that expands educational opportunities for typically marginalized students.

From CTE Courses to the World of Work

During the civic unrest and turmoil of 2012, students were encouraged to express their frustrations with "the system."[29] Most profound were their calls for career preparation and meaningful job opportunities. In the years following 2012, AUHSD started AIME to connect junior- and senior-level high school students to mentors from business, nonprofit, and civic sectors. Intro-

FIGURE 4.13 *Student participation in all iLab pathway courses, 2021–2022*

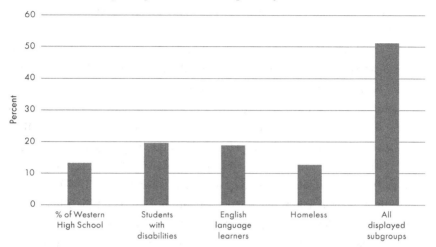

ducing young people to professionals in a variety of fields helps to open their eyes to career possibilities and start the process of developing access to social capital—the knowledge about how one moves from high school through postsecondary education and into a meaningful career. To date, more than 16,000 students have received mentoring support from AIME and its more than ninety-five partners.

AIME carries forward the work of CTE pathways to help students understand and potentially experience the world of work related to pathways. Students in grades 7 through 12 are supported with three tiers of mentoring: career exploration experiences, career mentoring series, and professional internship. All three tiers involve Anaheim Educational Collaborative partners and many entities beyond the collaborative. Often these are directly linked to pathways. For example, Kaiser Permanente provides mentoring to students in patient care pathways located in several schools. Similarly, Lennar Homes supports students in the residential and commercial construction pathway provided in three of the high schools.

Students may participate in AIME at three levels: (1) attending a speaker session to hear a professional discuss their field (often as a field trip to the business location), (2) a personalized mentoring experience involving meeting one-on-one or in small groups with professionals two to five times, and (3) an internship with a $600-per-semester stipend funded by grant money. Many of the students featured in our vignettes were accepted into internships that were pivotal to their postsecondary and career plans.

Available AIME data provide a broad-brush perspective on participation. Figure 4.14 shows that participation in AIME has varied widely among the district's comprehensive high schools over the past three years.

Notable peaks are the more than 25 percent of Anaheim High School's student body participating in one or more AIME activities during the 2019–2020 academic year and Savanna High School reaching 15 percent in 2021–2022. Participation diminished substantially during 2020–2021 when the schools and much of the community were closed because of COVID-19.

With large proportions of students benefiting from AIME, it is important to know how student subgroups are represented. The next four figures present comparisons for the four high schools with the greatest level of participation over the past three years—Anaheim, Magnolia, Savanna, and Western high schools. Recall that the low-income category is a supermajority (nearly 75 percent) of the district's total student population. Students are double-counted in AIME data, meaning that a student who is low income and an English language learner will be represented in the data in both categories.

Low-income and homeless Anaheim High School students have participated in AIME at a rate higher than or close to the participation rate for the

FIGURE 4.14 *AIME participation in AUHSD's comprehensive high schools*

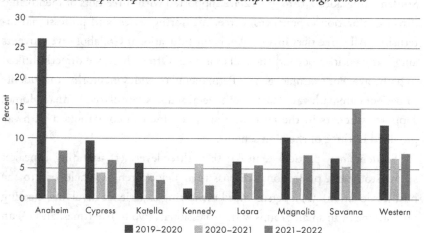

FIGURE 4.15 *Anaheim High School AIME participation by student subgroups*

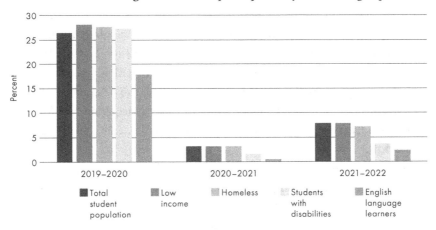

student body as a whole. SWD participated at nearly the same rate as homeless students in 2019–2020, but their rate declined over the three-year period. English language learner students remained noticeably below the overall school participation rate all three years.

Magnolia High School's participation patterns look similar to Anaheim's, though at a substantially lower overall rate in 2019–2020. (See figure 4.16.)

Savanna High School's participation is something of a mirror image of Anaheim's, with overall growth in participation from 2019–2020 to 2021–2022.

FIGURE 4.16 *Magnolia High School AIME participation by student subgroups*

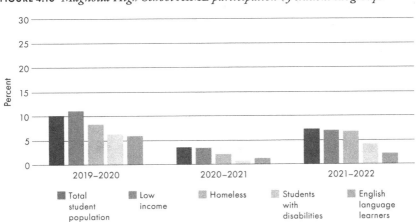

(See figure 4.17.) Most striking in the Savanna data is the disproportionately high participation among homeless students and SWD compared to the school's overall participation rate and the same student subgroups in other schools. Savanna had the highest participation rate during the COVID year with low-income and homeless students keeping pace with all students.

Western's participation patterns look most similar to Magnolia's, though its overall rate is somewhat higher. Notably, the participation rate for low-income students drops substantially below the overall rate in 2021–2022. (See figure 4.18.)

AIME is a promising strategy to connect student growth and purpose to the world of work. Creating these opportunities for students in an equitable fashion is an extremely challenging, complex enterprise. AIME involves numerous connections from counselors' offices to classrooms to AIME site coordinators and to the world of work. In short, numerous roles are required to be adept at three-level chess in support of AIME. Managing these connections requires a clear vision and persistence.

BUILDING THE AIME PROGRAM. AIME began with a small number of partnerships that Superintendent Matsuda and Mayor Tom Tait were able to create through a joint effort starting in 2017 with Kaiser Permanente as one of the original partners. Two key personnel were brought on board to grow the program. Scott Reindl serves as the coordinator for twenty-first-century career

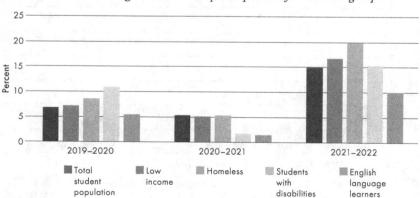

FIGURE 4.17 *Savanna High School AIME participation by student subgroups*

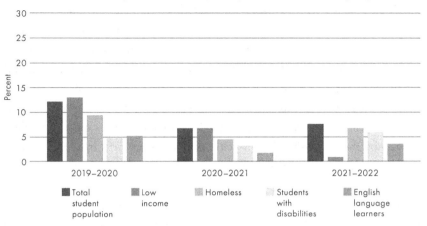

FIGURE 4.18 *Western High School AIME participation by student subgroups*

readiness, and Mary Jo (MJ) Cooke is the AIME program director, one of several new positions needed to operationalize the program.

The AIME program director has primary responsibility for finding new partners to serve as speakers, mentors, and internship sites and for supporting ongoing partners. She adopted a strategy of creating buzz within the community as each partner comes on board. Publicizing inspiring work within the school district has created a situation in which potential new partners seek out the director to learn how they can get involved, thus reducing the need for recruiting. Companies are interested in projecting a good citizenship image. AIME is effective in helping because, instead of monetary donations, they are seeking human involvement. Working with students is far more gratifying to the individuals involved than writing a check.

After AIME partners are committed, the director works on sustaining and growing their commitment through regular communication and staying up-to-date regarding mutual needs and interests. Her success is impressive, with over ninety-five partners to date and little attrition. Yet, as the number of partners grows so does the challenge of managing a program that stretches across many work types and individual and organizational personalities. Within the district, providing information, access, and opportunities for all the district's high school students is an enormous organizational task that requires understanding AIME as its own subsystem interacting with other internal and external systems.

Bringing students to AIME and AIME to students requires teacher leaders as advocates and organizers. To meet this need, AUHSD has created a position at each school with stipend compensation to serve as the work-based learning coordinator. The teacher serving in this role recruits students for AIME opportunities and is the school site contact person when the central office coordinator or AIME program director have an opportunity to match a partner with a school. Further personnel support is provided for AIME summer internships by teachers, again paid by stipend, who supervise student interns by meeting with them weekly to discuss progress in their jobs and meet regularly with internship supervisors in the field to check on progress and performance.

AIME personnel recognize that the program could reach students more equitably. Their efforts to have school educators such as special education case managers, coordinators for English language learners, and counselors to engage students in AIME have not yet borne fruit to the extent they would like. This is an area in which more teachers may need to see how AIME fits into their conception of It—the vision, I—my role in operationalizing the vision, and We—how I work with others to make it happen.

> *Food for Thought 4.2*
> What are the extent and depth of partnerships in your district? Do higher education institutions and private enterprises see roles for themselves in educating secondary students? How might you connect more closely with your community?

THREE-LEVEL CHESS TO HELP STUDENTS FIND PURPOSE

Readers will recall from chapter 2 the three-level chess metaphor we used to explain how to think through coordinating community resources with district operations from the central office through schools and into classrooms. Cybersecurity and all of the CTE pathways, the iLab, AIME, and other programs intended to help develop student voice and purpose all require three-level chess perspectives and skills to remake students' educational experiences. Coordination within and among all three levels is important. We start with level three and work our way down.

Level Three: The District Office Bridging to Resources

Superintendent Matsuda led the way in building key relationships at level three when he partnered with Mayor Tom Tait to signal to the broader community that AUHSD and the City of Anaheim were pursuing a common purpose—making schooling more important to adolescents while striving to have graduates take their places in strengthening the community. Nearly ten years after the initial commitment to making this difference for youth and the community, we are able to demonstrate this vision coming to fruition through districtwide data and graduate and community testimonials. But there are more pieces on the third level of the chessboard than local government.

Private enterprises—for-profit and nonprofit—were recruited to become additional powerful pieces. Matsuda generated key initial commitments from organizations willing to work with students and a long-term, deep partnership with entrepreneur Tim Nguyen. As in the case of cybersecurity, private-sector partners helped reverse-engineer new CTE pathways that fit the local context and opened doors to twenty-first-century careers that could not have been imagined when today's graduates entered kindergarten. Career pathways so new are likely beyond reach of many AUHSD teachers, making the local community colleges another set of key pieces on the chessboard. They joined the partnership by providing instruction in dual-enrollment courses that would give students the technical skills needed to enter fields that spur their interests and have the promise of a prosperous future.

With foundational partnerships in place and an understanding of key practices, such as those embedded in the Anaheim Educational Collaborative, the district office (DO) needed to expand partnership development at level three while building infrastructure and processes at level two.

Level Two: The District Office Supporting the Schools

Full-time curriculum specialists and part-time 5Cs coaches (two periods coaching, three periods teaching) are personnel Matsuda developed and worked with prior to becoming superintendent. With them in place and learning how to function with the schools before conception of the CPSF, they are a source of high potential on the level-two chessboard. They address a three-part challenge: (1) communicating to teachers, counselors, support staff, and site administrators the nature and purpose of community resources that will help strengthen youth voice and purpose; (2) illustrating how both technical skills and twenty-first-century skills enable students to take advantage of new opportunities being generated; and (3) guiding changes in teacher practice to meet changed learning needs that flow from the CPSF. Curriculum specialists and 5Cs coaches in turn require support from DO directors who manage budgets, bring in resources, and provide professional learning to all of these teachers on special assignments.

One 5Cs coach per school site and six curriculum specialists will never be able to reach more than 1,200 teachers districtwide. AUHSD relies on department chairs and new site positions to lend strength to the level-two chessboard. Additional teacher leaders have been given time to coordinate AIME efforts on site and energize additional programs that bring resources and opportunities into classrooms. Department chairs and teacher leaders in other roles learn at the DO the purposes and practices of programs they support at their sites while providing feedback to DO personnel on implementation challenges and needs. The Capstone project described in chapter 2 provides a vivid illustration of level-two play.

Moving from traditional grading and standardized testing to understanding how well students are developing integrated technical and twenty-first-century skills requires a new approach to student assessment and monitoring school and district progress. Curriculum specialists with assistance from directors created the concept of performance task assessments (PTAs) to demonstrate 5Cs skills, different types of student voice, and content knowledge. These student performances are intended to be meaningful work aligned with the world beyond school boundaries and should occur at least once per quarter. Performance tasks consistent across sections of the same course serve as accountability for curriculum implementation and provide data to understand how well students are progressing toward finding their voice and purpose. Curriculum specialists and 5Cs coaches work with other teacher leaders and teachers in general to understand and implement PTAs.

But how are data from PTAs collected? Recall the portfolio from chapter 2. Students are expected to build and maintain a portfolio that contains their reflections on their learning progress—in the classroom and in the community—to be used when they have their Capstone experience at the end of junior high and high school. This is an important source of data because it tracks students' understanding of their own development and what they need next in their education.

Accessing data from 1,200 teachers and 27,000 students to chart progress toward CPSF goals requires a database that is user-friendly for students and teachers who are entering these data and site and DO leaders who need to know school and district progress. Chess at levels two and three are combined in AUHSD to create eKadence, a new learning management system that facilitates data collection and analysis.[30] Tim Nguyen has donated his company's time and resources to develop eKadence to meet the specific needs of the CPSF. Students' portfolios are created in eKadence, thus providing teachers, principals, and DO staff access to stored qualitative data, particularly students' reflections on their learning. PTAs and other teacher assessments are assigned and graded through eKadence using rubrics that require teachers to describe students' performance in terms of technical skills and twenty-first-century skills. AUHSD is developing reports from eKadence that can illustrate student performance across class sections, schoolwide, and districtwide, while creating opportunities for narrower deep dives to determine how well curriculum and instruction are reaching students in various ways.

Level One: Schools and Classrooms

Resources and personnel from levels two and three are intended to guide and support teachers toward achieving CPSF goals for all students every day. Classrooms are, of course, essential for teaching technical skills and twenty-first-century skills, but they can also supercharge nonclassroom opportunities such as the iLab or AIME mentoring and internships in two ways. Students develop their motivation to be curious and try new ideas when invited to do so. 5Cs development provides an ideal mechanism for broadening students' awareness of what school can do for them. For example, a teacher working with students to improve their collaborative skills might give them opportunities to be persuasive and reflective with one another in small groups working on content such as mathematics. While using evidence to support their own ideas, they would be listening to other group members to identify the strongest solution. This kind of teamwork is an invaluable skill working in a nonschool setting to write code for a specific task, figuring out how to get healthy food to communities without supermarkets, or getting and giving feedback that strengthens a public presentation. The second means teachers have to leverage district partnerships and resources is to bring students' experiences with CTE pathways or AIME into classroom learning. For example, a student in the biotechnology career pathway might have learned a specific application that could be brought to the biology classroom for illustration. This would be a gratifying opportunity for the presenting student and might motivate others to explore biotechnology.

Teachers and principals well informed about and strongly affected by all the efforts occurring at levels two and three will be better equipped to bring the CPSF to life in classrooms. Instructional leaders at the site—administrative team members, department chairs, coaches, and other teacher leaders—are essential players at level one. Their primary tasks are to prevent teachers from being isolated and to help them through the inevitable struggles that they will face as they strive to change classroom practices.

> **Food for Thought 4.3**
> Does three-level chess make sense in practical terms in your district? What new players might you want to recruit as partners in opposition to the status quo?

Summary: Redesigning School Content

Numerous partnerships have changed what it feels like to go to school in AUHSD while maintaining or improving student performance on traditional outcome measures. Dual enrollment, innovative CTE pathways linked to mentoring and internships beyond school boundaries, portfolios students curate to display their best work and metacognition, and a culminating Capstone experience to present the portfolio are examples of substantial changes over the past ten years that have reshaped AUHSD graduates' school experiences. More examples are listed in appendix B. The single largest program in support of the CPSF—Community Schools—is discussed in chapter 6. We focus next on the development of student voice in classrooms and beyond.

ELEVATING STUDENT VOICE WHILE DEVELOPING LIFE PURPOSE

When we discussed affective skill development in chapters 1 and 2, we made general reference to Savanna High School. Teachers and administration created the first Capstone and a precursor to the 5Cs, which they labeled "student learning capacities." The innovation of incorporating affective skills into teaching outcomes struggled to take hold schoolwide. English teacher Mike Switzer and principal Manuel Colon decided to pilot a culminating high school learning reflection with Switzer's senior English students as a means to capture which affective skills students had learned and what it meant to them. After the successful pilot, they implemented the Savanna High School Capstone project schoolwide.

The Capstone was developed by a team of teachers Switzer led with enthusiastic support from Principal Colon. Even with strong principal support and substantial teacher energy, initiating and spreading an innovation is never easy, as Switzer explains:

> That pilot year they had to turn in one thing that represented them as critical thinkers [and] one thing that represented them as being globally aware . . . [T]he students really struggled to find the pieces . . . The vision of the school . . . we had on the walls at the school was not happening inside the four walls of classrooms. Manuel and I put our heads together and we thought, "Okay, let's do this for all seniors the next year."
>
> What we did is we put the student learning capacities out in front and we started doing some lesson design work around [them] . . . [Instead of looking to test scores] we said, "What can we do to make our kids better communicators? What can we do to make them better collaborators?" We were much more intentional as teachers . . . It was really on the shoulders of the English teachers, I think, at that point. And what we definitely found out that first year, which would have been the 2012–2013 school year, is the artifacts that we were seeing . . . were almost all from English classes. And they were almost all student essays. I think at the time we were still in that mind-set that presentations were things that you did at the end of the year, like you did those after [testing].
>
> We found such value in the process that the following year . . . we did make it schoolwide. What I mean by that is, we started to build the learning capacities and to work from ninth grade to twelfth grade. It was definitely on the radar, and I'll use the phrase *on the radar* because we still weren't totally intentional about it. [With colleagues on the professional development team]

we would work with [teachers] to try to embed the learning capacities into their lesson design, so that they would be intentional. Part of that process we tried to define what a performance task was, and we asked all the teachers to do two or three performance tasks a year with their students. And the hope was that, at the conclusion of the performance tasks, the students would do some reflecting on the student learning capacities.[31]

More than ten years after initiation of the Savanna Capstone, students, with guidance from a teacher, select their most meaningful work across the curriculum of their four high school years and, within the framework of the 5Cs, reflect on how this work helped them develop into the young people they are today. As graduation approaches, seniors present their portfolios and discuss their mastery of key skills—including the 5Cs—and knowledge they've acquired with a panel of teachers and volunteers from the school community. This public discussion of students' learning sharpens their perspective—their voice—and often leads to brief discussions about their future.

As we write this in the 2022–2023 academic year, the rest of AUHSD's twenty schools, including the junior high schools, magnet schools, and alternative education schools, are piloting their own portfolio and Capstone experiences based on design work they conducted the previous spring. Schools are encouraged to design Capstones that are age- and context-appropriate with a clear understanding that the process is intended to generate student reflection about what matters most to them as they have learned technical skills and twenty-first-century skills. Developing student voice and purpose are prominent features of the entire process. AUHSD's theory of change regarding the portfolio and Capstone is captured in figure 4.19.

IMPLEMENTING PORTFOLIOS AND THE CAPSTONE. All students should graduate with the knowledge and skills in academic subjects that enable them to transition successfully to higher education and rewarding careers. But academic knowledge and skills alone are inadequate for success in life beyond high school. Parents, employers, and college and university educators recognize that students must develop their own personal mastery and interpersonal skills (twenty-first-century skills) to thrive in education, work, and career. It is the twenty-first-century skills that give students the tools to make the best use of their academic preparation. The challenge is to move beyond recognizing

FIGURE 4.19 *AUHSD theory of change embedded in the Capstone program*

Shared Vision	Performance Task Assessment System	Capstone Program Structure
AUHSD's shared vision, driven by *student voice and purpose*, *21st century skills*, and *technical skills* provides a collective framework that will position students for success in education, careers, and life.	Performance Task Assessments provide students opportunities to engage in meaningful, purposeful work; to develop independence and self-direction; to think deeply in relevant academic contexts; and to develop voice and agency through their learning.	A schoolwide portfolio structure ensures that ALL students receive access to relevant, meaningful learning experiences that support academic, social, and emotional wellbeing.
Each school's unique Capstone Program aligns the school's vision and values to students' everyday classroom experiences.	All students are provided multiple opportunities within each class to engage in meaningful, relevant performance tasks that allow them to develop voice, the 5Cs, and technical skills.	Students reflect upon and showcase meaningful tasks throughout in all classes through each year of schooling.

The Capstone structure, anchored by each school's Performance Task Assessment System, will bring to life AUHSD's vision of providing all students an engaging curriculum centered by voice and purpose, 21st century skills, and technical skills.

AUHSD's Capstone Program will ensure that all students are provided relevant and engaging learning experiences that prepare them for meaningful, purposeful lives.

Source: Anaheim Union High School District: *The Capstone Playbook.*

the need for such skills into making them important in the daily educational experiences of all students.

Part of elevating the importance of these skills is showing in concrete ways how teachers' classroom choices and moves affect students' learning. When teachers put in place twenty-first-century skills learning, students require opportunities to reflect on their learning so that teachers are able to assess progress. The portfolio and Capstone structures are intentionally designed to make students' twenty-first-century skills growth visible to students and teachers alike and show how they are integrated with technical skills learning in a manner that elevates youth voice and purpose.

Having each school develop its own Capstone experience preserves autonomy and choice at the school level and allows schools to align how students think about their learning with the school's vision. Students' Capstone experiences are built from portfolios of their best work that demonstrate their growth in technical skills and twenty-first-century skills. The PTAs discussed above and developed by teachers within their content areas anchor the portfolio because teachers and students go on record regarding what the student has learned and what it means up to that moment in the classroom experience. Portfolios also include students' chosen work samples, which may come from the classroom, a mentoring experience, civic engagement, internship in a career field, or some integration of learning that takes place in the classroom and the community simultaneously. Most important is the student's reflection on growth and development and how that is propelling them toward a calling, an emerging purpose. Providing a Capstone experience at the end of the academic year is a commitment to students that they will have the opportunity to communicate their aspirations, growth, and future progress. The individualized nature of the portfolio and Capstone is also a commitment by AUHSD educators to know and understand every student's story as they progress through the system.

CONCLUSION

The programs we have described, the ways they fit into district operations, and the students they serve speak to the complication and complexity involved in moving education from focusing on tests to focusing on life. The work represented by CPSF core educational programs is essential to making US schooling engaging and empowering. Without such efforts, social mobility remains a myth, except for the lucky few able to break free from the US education status quo.

District leaders and policy makers will need to figure out students' needs and appropriate solutions for their own contexts. Our intent is to assist by explaining how the CPSF works for students in practice, showing evidence of success, and providing key information for building similar programs. Educating for purposeful life will have nuanced variations to fit different student populations, community assets, and policy-level aspirations.

> ### Food for Thought 4.4
> In what ways is student voice expressed and heard within your district's schools? What about in the broader community?

We hope that our depiction of signature CPSF programs appears in sharp contrast to the status quo in most school districts. At the same time, we want to acknowledge that change at this scope and scale takes time, focus, and perseverance. Systems and people will be stressed. This is why in chapter 5 we explore a form of mindfulness consistent with the 5Cs and effective for coping with the pressures that come from participating in a new approach to educating adolescents.

TAKING STOCK

Reading about programs that have been years in development can seem overwhelming. We hope, however, that this chapter has inspired you to think in new ways about how educators can better address the needs of the whole student, the whole person. Assuming you are more inspired than not, it might be helpful to reflect on the following:

1. What kinds of changes in the educational experience are most important to your students right now?
   - Which one or two changes would you like to begin working on in the short term?
   - Which two to four changes do you believe would likely follow from the first one or two?
2. What is your school board's orientation toward making positive change?
   - How might you go through a learning process with your district's school board so they can put their energy behind making positive change?
3. Who are the like-minded community partners within your district's boundaries who would welcome the opportunity to make a positive change in education?
   - How might grants such as those from GEAR UP help to fuel your effort to make students' educational experiences more engaging and impactful?

CHAPTER 5

MINDFULNESS AND THE FIFTH C

> The moment we recognize that the self is not something ready-made, but something in continuous formation through choice of action, the whole situation clears up.
>
> —JOHN DEWEY[1]

ONE HUNDRED YEARS before the CPSF and forty years before Maslow's hierarchy, Dewey captured two essential elements for the CPSF in the short quotation that leads off this chapter.[2] The CPSF strives to make the creation of selfhood the focus of secondary education, just as Dewey advocated as a leader of the Progressive movement in education.[3] Today, we think of selfhood as student voice and purpose. When students can pursue the career interests they have, their self—their purpose—is clearer to them. Achieving classroom goals means that students understand how content aligns with their purpose. The second point is about motivation, specifically self-actualization. We interpret Dewey's notion of "choice of action" as a process for creating the self to be exactly our aspiration for students' learning experiences. In secondary school and beyond, AUHSD graduates are given choices and take actions in pursuit of those interests embedded in their identities. They take control of their futures as they self-actualize.

We focus this chapter on individual control of emotion and impulse vital to fulfillment in family, work, and life. And we emphasize the fifth C—Compassion—because self-control and hard work without compassion are merely robotic. As we claim throughout the book, *integration* of twenty-first-century skills with technical skills is a necessary condition for success in school, at work, at home, and in the community. These tenets apply not only to students but also to the educators who serve them.

THE ROAD TO MINDFULNESS

In 2013, when then Anaheim mayor Tom Tait and district administrator Matsuda convened students in small groups to hear their concerns about their city, the students expressed the need for more mentoring from business leaders and support for the 4Cs.[4] Matsuda remembers a few students who spoke assertively about adding a fifth C for caring or character. One young man spoke passionately and said, "The Nazis were brilliant in the 4Cs. They almost conquered Europe and Russia and wanted world domination for their Aryan race. What they lacked is empathy for others. They just didn't care about them. Four Cs are not enough." Another student said, "Today there are a lot of selfish, greedy people who go to top universities but who lack morals. They might make a lot of money but are corrupt. I agree, 4Cs don't cut it. Why not try *character*?" Tait and Matsuda were impressed and added a fifth C for character, which later became Compassion. The shift was motivated by mindfulness training that began in AUHSD in 2016.

At the end of his second year as superintendent, Matsuda traveled to upstate New York to visit his old friend Dr. Home H. C. Nguyen, who has adopted the simple moniker Dr. Home. Recently completing his doctorate on the effect of mindfulness practices in organizational leadership and culture, Dr. Home was uniquely positioned to advise Matsuda and his team.

Dr. Home is a refugee boat person from Vietnam who narrowly escaped with his family as a young boy in the 1980s. Dr. Home and Matsuda became friends early in their respective careers in the mid-1990s, serving immigrant communities in very different ways. As Matsuda was getting started as an English teacher, Dr. Home was majoring in acting at California State University, Northridge. Already socially and politically active, he created a theater troupe that portrayed the refugee experience. Club of Noodles used humor to convey poignant refugee stories about and for the Vietnamese community. Matsuda and Dr. Home connected through his effort to heal the legacy of trauma that children and adults were living through.

By the time their friendship was rekindled, Dr. Home had cofounded a mindfulness retreat on a twenty-acre farm leased from a group of Episcopal nuns. His client list by this time included several *Fortune* 500 executives. Fresh out of graduate school at Columbia University, Dr. Home was immersed in the research on mental health conditions of youth and the disturbing growing prevalence of suicidal ideation, alienation, anxiety, and depression among youth. Dr. Home's understanding of complex organizations coupled with insights into low-income, immigrant adolescent needs provided an essential perspective for Matsuda's aspirations for AUHSD students.

Their summer 2016 conversation began with a ten-minute meditation exercise Dr. Home called "Loving-Kindness." Matsuda emerged feeling at peace, comfortable, and grateful in the moment. They then turned to the subject of the mental state of adolescents. Matsuda conjured images of AUHSD students living in garages, motels, or on the streets and lamented how far they must be from the tranquil space and frame of mind he was in at that moment. Because AUHSD was in the shadow of Disneyland, Matsuda referenced the farm where his conversation with Dr. Home was taking place and commented wryly, "This place, this beautiful, reflective spot is actually better than Disneyland." They laughed. Then Dr. Home responded, "It's really about dopamine, isn't it?"

The pleasure, satisfaction, and motivation that dopamine registers in the brain are rare commodities for youth who experience mechanical, stultifying educational experiences during the day and social media shaming, blaming, and bullying in their afterschool hours.[5] Dr. Home pointed out that although there are many causes for the increased occurrence of mental illness, academics generally agree that the rise coincides with growing access to social media in the past twenty years.[6]

Opening a social media app is like playing a slot machine, Dr. Home explained. Opening the app generates spontaneous results—either pleasurable or disappointing. Similar to roulette, the house wins in the long run, meaning that as a source of dopamine—that is, positive reinforcement—social media is a bad bet for most youth.

Matsuda pointed out another way in which secondary students' self-concept and motivation were under attack—standardized testing. The mechanization of the teaching process through an overemphasis on preparing for and taking standardized tests crowded out opportunities to reach students and educate the whole child. Twenty years of focusing on English language arts and math to the exclusion of the rest of the curriculum had stifled teachers' ability to engage students with the spark of learning and inquiry based on real-world problem-solving. High-stakes testing, in Matsuda's view, had undermined schools as a pathway to the American Dream and emphasized the sorting process of schooling, actually leaving students behind more than helping them. The results were antidemocratic on many dimensions. Matsuda summed up his perspective by saying, "We are at a dangerous inflection point because kids are losing faith in schools. They are checking out."

They turned to a favorite author, Viktor Frankl, as they considered what to do about a disheartening situation. In *Man's Search for Meaning*, Frankl wrote about overcoming helplessness by recognizing choices open to us. Frankl's incarceration at Auschwitz and his observation of those who perished and those who survived taught him that even in the most dire circumstances, human beings have choices they can make, and such choices are empowering. As he developed his own brand of psychotherapy before and after Auschwitz, Frankl claimed that most apparent neuroses were not mental diseases. Instead, psychological troubles were symptomatic of helplessness. Frankl treated patients by helping them find purpose and taking action to achieve their purpose. This simple idea of finding purpose in life and taking action to achieve it powers the CPSF. Dr. Home made the point that in the space where choice lives is the essence of mindfulness. He helped Matsuda recognize mindfulness as a critical tool to help students and the educators around them see choices within their grasp as they identified their purpose and pursued it. Maslow would call the result self-actualization. But Frankl, based on seeing emaciated concentration camp victims give away bread to help others saw ultimate purpose in transcending the self:[7]

> Science has confirmed what the Eastern philosophers have practiced for generations—meditative practices allow one to control the synapse between stimulus and response. So much of our emotional response is programmed from childhood that we are triggered from toxic emotions we experienced as children. Mindfulness allows one to press the "pause button" and choose a different response; one grounded in kindness.
>
> —DR. HOME NGUYEN[8]

Frankl labeled his approach to therapy "Logotherapy." The Greek term *logos* refers to a rational explanation for the universe. Frankl advocated thinking rationally about emotional responses to be able to bring them under control and take hold of one's life. AUHSD's twenty-first-century adolescents need a modified approach to taking control of their lives. In the altered words, not the meaning, of one of the young people quoted at the beginning of this chapter, rationality without compassion is insufficient.

The following year, Dr. Home cofounded the MindKind Institute with professional partner Sarah Suatoni, a marriage and family therapist. Their purpose is to connect mind, body, and spirit through executive coaching and therapy. Suatoni summarizes their approach this way: "While mindfulness is to be present in the moment, a tool to use as a bridge between what you think and what you feel—MindKindness is the integration of the head and the heart."[9] Dr. Home made this point with Matsuda, that compassion and kindness needed to be woven into mindfulness to give it heart. He addresses the needs of the AUHSD student population and alignment with the CPSF by saying:

> MindKindness is a trauma-informed practice which allows people who have had traumatic mental distress to practice in a safe and affirming approach, often called somatic psychology. MindKindness is also a practice for building relationships and effective communication. It is a field of practice that engages organizations in a cultural transformation. This means that MindKindness is not just individual personal development, but also a trust building practice for healthy relationships in organizations.

The pieces came together. Matsuda was able to see how mindfulness with compassion could build cohesion among the It, We, and I for AUHSD educators to help transform the district. Infusing mindfulness into teaching via the 5Cs would help students dealing with anxieties driven by their life circumstances to pause long enough before acting to leave negative, antisocial behaviors behind and work toward their purpose. Practicing the fifth C—Compassion—would have a particularly profound effect on building a sense of community within secondary schools and the broader world.

Food for Thought 5.1

What strategies are you using in your school or district to help students cope with stress from their daily lives? How well is it working? Is there a need for a MindKindness-type of approach?

A WORK IN PROGRESS

Matsuda was filled with enthusiasm for mindfulness and asked Dr. Home if he would train AUHSD teachers and students. His response was that organizational transformation requires commitment from the top:

> You can't just impose MindKindness from the top down and expect there to be buy-in or sustainable growth. Change within an organization requires the commitment from the chief executive and all of the cabinet members. Then we must invite the most influential and early adopters at all levels of the organization to participation. If you want to make real change, you have to be willing to do it for yourself and all of your leaders.[10]

Matsuda agreed and decided that Dr. Home and Suatoni could help with the shift in organization culture he was seeking. Author Sharon Kruse commented:

> [E]ffective leadership practice requires that people understand themselves, the people they work with, the communities they serve, and the organizations they lead. This is hardly a bold statement . . . Yet, each of those tasks—understanding ourselves, those around us, and the structures and systems that comprise our schools—can be daunting, and requires continuous, ongoing, reflective attention and practice. One can spend a lifetime figuring out who they are. Equally difficult, if not even more so, is the challenge of knowing and understanding the perspectives of teachers, staff, students, and families that make up a school community.[11]

Kruse categorizes mindfulness for school leadership in three ways: (1) contemplative, (2) cognitive, and (3) organizational. AUHSD focuses its mindfulness work in the first two categories. Contemplative mindfulness aligns with Senge's idea of personal mastery, a concept Matsuda strongly emphasizes with leaders. Cognitive mindfulness reinforces ontological humility as individuals pause in heated debate to consider their point of view through It, We, and I. We recognize that making fundamental changes in educational practices puts school and district leaders under stress. Leadership development that includes mindfulness as a means to reducing stress and improving job performance is an important element for initiating and sustaining positive change.

Since 2017, MindKind has provided district school leaders with training in self-awareness and relational awareness in ways typically not available to public school educators. Highlights include leadership coaching, workshops, and programs that focus on emotional intelligence and conscious communication.[12] Surveys of AUHSD administrators who have experienced MindKind professional development confirm that MindKind has helped them develop the ability to use the synapse between stimulus and response so that they are able to practice the 5Cs themselves and contribute to a culture of belonging and compassion within AUHSD.

Mindfulness for Students

Matsuda and Dr. Home's original aspiration was to bring mindfulness training and practice to all AUHSD students through teachers' design of classroom experiences. A local nonprofit—Brian Ton's Illumination Institute—has the capacity to teach mindfulness to teachers and parents in English, Spanish, and Vietnamese. Over five years, Illumination Institute has educated over four hundred volunteer teachers and hundreds of parents in basic mindfulness practices, including meditation, with the intent of passing this learning on to students in classrooms and at home. Ton's group has also worked with student leaders and teachers interested in creating elective courses with a mindfulness curriculum. A local university surveyed 5,000 AUHSD students to determine the impact of bringing mindfulness into classrooms and schools. The researchers found inverse correlations between mindfulness practices experienced by students and three indicators of psychological distress and a positive correlation for executive functioning, displayed in table 5.1.

Preliminary results in the table are from 2022. The district will continue to find ways to infuse mindfulness into students' classroom experiences as an important support for developing voice and purpose on the path to a purposeful life. Helping teachers engage in mindfulness practices for themselves and with

TABLE 5.1 *Survey results correlating mindfulness practices and indicators of student mental health*

	Depression	Anxiety	Stress	Executive functioning
Students reporting mindfulness practices	−0.57*	−0.60*	−0.62*	0.69*

*$p < .01$.

their students is daunting in the face of all the demands of daily teaching and the ways in which the CPSF is changing the nature of education in AUHSD. We offer the following excerpt of a letter from an AUHSD teacher to mindfulness trainers to show the potential of mindfulness to change school culture and, by extension, the trajectory of students facing substantial life challenges:

Dear Ms. Suatoni and Mr. Yuan,
I was encouraged to write to you to fill you in on some of the remarkable experiences that are happening at our school. My principal, Mr. Chau, mentioned the MindKind Cohort that many emerging leaders on campus are a part of now. [I see] a connection to the experiences I have witnessed. I hope you find my examples encouraging as coaches of the work that is changing the camaraderie and morale at our school.

My name is Katrina, and this is my eighteenth year as an English teacher at Magnolia High School . . . This year, I also have the privilege of serving as our Community School Teacher Lead. We have had all kinds of leaders on our campus, and many have come and gone. Our school is unique and has challenges that aren't common to other schools. Our [staff attrition] rate is high. [But] things have changed this year partnering with our new leadership . . . [Our principal] Mr. Chau . . . is a huge advocate of MindKind and the work you are leading. The techniques that are coached are valued and implemented by him. The tone of our culture has changed.

Mr. Chau and his team went into every class at the beginning of the year to introduce themselves and give a presentation about expectations and guidelines and to explain to kids why those boundaries were in place. I always like to get feedback from the kids after the admin visit. They mentioned to me, "It feels different. It's strict, but everyone has been really kind." They are secure with having boundaries in place because of the way the administration speaks with them. Our kids know they are cared for. This has branched out to the teachers, our security, and beyond. This mentality has had a rippling effect that has created a sense of calm and safety on our campus.

We start every staff meeting with mindfulness. The focus is different and I don't think we have ever had meetings where people have been . . . so engaged and encouraging of each other. At our weekly cabinet meeting, one of our staff members became upset and overwhelmed because of something in the news [that related to] her elderly mother. She broke down. She was asking us to move on, but I watched Mr. Chau read the room, take a minute, and pause to call for a five-minute break. It was so wonderful to witness empathy in such a caring, professional way. It's these little moments of pause and identifying the need that really tells our faculty that they are individually valued and cared for.

A standout experience for me was on the day I returned to school after being out for a week. Mr. Chau offered to have my class covered by an extra sub so I could have some time to catch up, or if I just needed time to rest. I think I may have asked him to repeat himself because I was so shocked. In all my years at Magnolia, I have never been treated with such empathy . . . [and] with the kind of humanity I strive to show to my students. Although I declined the offer because I missed my kids, this inspired my work even more because I was supported and felt more capable of supporting my students. I would do the same for our administration if they needed anything. It's this type of work environment that I believe helps us thrive as educators, and I know I am not the only one who has stories like mine. I am so grateful to you both for the work that you are doing and I know I will want to be a part of learning the next MindKind Cohort.[13]

> **Food for Thought 5.2**
>
> How many teachers in your school or district intentionally treat their students with kindness and compassion? How many would claim that school and district leaders treat teachers with kindness and compassion?

CONCLUSION

Growing students' capacity to use twenty-first-century skills as embodied in the 5Cs is one of the greatest instructional challenges presented by the CPSF. Although many teachers address students' affective needs intuitively, naturally, and with charisma, some do not. Asking secondary teachers to teach their content in inspiring and effective ways while engaging students' mind, body, and spirit is external to the preparation most young teachers have had and is alien to the experience of some veterans. Curriculum specialists, 5Cs coaches, and school leaders would likely agree that incorporating the 5Cs into daily teaching across all classrooms is very much a work in progress. The central puzzle is helping teachers understand how to activate the 5Cs and encouraging them to try.

Mindfulness in AUHSD is one avenue for solving the puzzle. The key is alignment among what leaders say they expect from teachers, leaders' modeling the behaviors and mind-sets they expect from teachers, and sustaining emphasis on the 5Cs and students' affective development generally. We have preliminary data that show when teachers succeed in their role as mindful educators, students benefit. We do not yet have data to demonstrate teachers' responses to the mindfulness education that has occurred so far, but Katrina's letter indicates great promise for the future.

Mindfulness is a framework, an approach to improving oneself and relating to colleagues and students. Coupled with compassion, mindfulness can soften the rough edges created by the stress inherent in secondary school education and lead to better outcomes. Yet, it is but one of many ways in which AUHSD educators need to develop themselves to achieve the vision and goals of the CPSF. Chapter 6 explains the central role of professional learning aligned with elevating youth voice and purpose.

TAKING STOCK

As social-emotional learning (SEL) has taken hold in districts across the country, we notice that it often stands apart as something extra in students' educational experiences. At the same time, we have heard teachers say, "What about SEL for me? I am under stress just like my students." These experiences tell us that strategies that help teachers and students manage their emotional or affective responses to stressors and challenges need to be more comprehensive. The following questions may help you think through how you might like to address the affective learning of both teachers and students:

1. How is teachers' mental health supported and nurtured in your school district?
   - Are teachers more inclined to be full of energy and optimism, or is it more common for them to appear to be "soldiering along"?
2. What do you notice about teachers' affect compared to that of students?
   - Do students key off their teachers' unspoken communications and respond in ways counter to what we hope for in classrooms?
3. What sort of attention to sustaining energized optimism will be necessary as you work to initiate and sustain positive change?

CHAPTER 6

TEACHER PROFESSIONAL LEARNING

> If you are not in the arena getting your ass kicked on occasion, I am not interested in or open to your feedback.
>
> —BRENÉ BROWN[1]

BRENÉ BROWN'S POPULAR DISTILLATION and updating of a famous Theodore Roosevelt speech captures teachers' perspectives. Teachers are in the arena every day, an arena that is shaped by the context and culture of their professional lives. The great majority of them are engaging, connecting, relating, listening, affirming, motivating, and loving the nation's 50 million K–12 students in their classrooms. Faith in the mission of public schools and the belief that, through them, young people can reach their own aspirations, purpose, and pathway to the American Dream are patriotic and essential to teaching effectiveness. Yet, teaching is a hard job subject to relentless criticism from sectors of parents; the business community; and local, state, and federal policy makers. Teaching may be the most underappreciated profession in America. The combined pressures of the need to improve classroom practices, intense public scrutiny, and external shocks such as the COVID-19 pandemic drive teachers out of the profession at alarming rates.[2] Professional learning that grows teacher talent improves their self-efficacy, motivating them to stay in teaching while benefiting their students. Addressing teachers' affective and cognitive needs and aspirations in an integrated fashion mirrors educating students for purposeful life.

Those who would help teachers improve their performance earn their credibility through experience. Teachers respect peers who are teaching alongside them, veterans who have taught in their settings, and professionals who understand what it means to stand tall in their arena day after day for a whole career. AUHSD has structured professional learning with teachers' perspectives clearly in mind, along with another admonition from Brown and Roosevelt—to dare greatly. AUHSD's professional learning recognizes teachers' needs to identify and pursue their aspirations as educators while building the skills and knowledge required to teach in new and more effective ways.

The CPSF is designed to develop each student's voice and purpose and prepare them for a meaningful world of work grounded in compassion for others. CPSF goals liberate teachers from the decades-old yoke of teaching to a test to focus on what matters most to students striving to take their place in their community and build a better world. For nearly all teachers, the CPSF has allowed them to reconnect with their own purpose—their "I" in Kofman's terms. It helps them to return to the reasons why they entered the profession in the first place. Achieving CPSF goals with all students requires professional learning opportunities that help teachers cocreate and design experiences that go far beyond test scores and unleash students' passion, creativity, and productivity.

> *Food for Thought 6.1*
> What does the teaching arena look like in your district? What are the strongest supports? What are the greatest threats?

PROFESSIONAL LEARNING AVENUES

According to Richard Elmore:

> [T]he existing structure and culture of schools seems better designed to resist learning and improvement than to enable it . . . [T]here are few portals through which new knowledge about teaching and learning can enter schools; few structures or processes in which teachers and administrators can assimilate, adapt, and polish new ideas and practices; and few sources of assistance for those who are struggling to understand the connection between

the academic performance of their students and the practices in which they engage . . .

For every increment of performance I demand from you, I have an equal responsibility to provide you with the capacity to meet that expectation. Likewise, for every investment you make in my skill and knowledge, I have a reciprocal responsibility to demonstrate some new increment in performance.[3]

We quote Elmore before describing AUHSD's approach to professional learning in detail because he explains in different terms that schools and districts are not naturally learning organizations under the status quo. Two decades of test scores as the essential driver in school systems have greatly inhibited learning, creativity, and innovation. The general puzzle for leaders is complicated by a long history of communicating high expectations for teachers combined with low quality or missing professional learning. Yet, Elmore provides a solution of mutual responsibility in which high expectations from leadership are supported with the professional learning necessary to meet them, and teachers are responsible for follow-through that implements improved classroom practices.

Professional learning in AUHSD embraces Elmore's concept of mutual responsibility in three strategic steps: (1) curriculum specialists collaborate with 5Cs coaches, (2) school- and districtwide structured professional learning is designed and disseminated from the district office (DO), and (3) teacher-teacher coaching and learning occur in all schools on a regular basis. The approach resembles three-level chess within the district because curriculum specialists (level two) must understand CPSF imperatives (e.g., teaching civic engagement) and opportunities outside school (e.g., business and nonprofit workforce partnerships—collectively, level three), while being mindful of current curriculum (level two) and pedagogical practices (level one). Curriculum specialists develop skills, knowledge, and dispositions of the 5Cs coaches (level two) who work directly with classroom teachers (level one). In addition to the curriculum specialists and 5Cs coaches, teacher leaders are empowered to innovate in ways that fuel the CPSF and help their colleagues discover more effective ways to elevate student voice and purpose while teaching technical skills at the highest levels. The sections that follow explain how the different components of professional learning function.

The DO Professional Learning Shop

> We are not about a one and done. It's got to be ongoing, a thematic approach. Our modeling is essential.
> —DIANA FUJIMOTO, COORDINATOR, PROFESSIONAL LEARNING[4]

In her characteristic style, Fujimoto explains three basic principles that guide professional learning design and implementation at the DO. These principles are intended to filter into the school sites via the 5Cs coaches, through direct contact between curriculum specialists and school sites, and via professional learning for department chairs and other teacher leaders. Fujimoto places heavy emphasis on collaboration, first with her team of nine curriculum specialists and then with the 5Cs coaches from each of the district's schools. The teams focus their design and implementation efforts strategically on the most important current district initiative to drive the CPSF forward. In 2022–2023, the focus is on implementation of each school's Capstone project, an example we use to illustrate how professional learning works in AUHSD.

In addition to their duties managing curricula for the district, curriculum specialists are essential players in initiating professional learning that addresses the capacity-building side of Elmore's mutual responsibility. They meet weekly with Fujimoto to design professional learning that occurs in the monthly day-long sessions required for all 5Cs coaches. Recalling that 5Cs coaches teach three periods and coach two, their professional learning occurs on two levels simultaneously. On one level, they are learning how to implement innovative classroom practices *as teachers*. At the same time, they are expected to apply their learning and experience as they *coach teachers* in ways that support their implementation of improved practices across curricula. Their teacher leadership requires deep understanding of the instructional core and pedagogical content knowledge within and beyond their own content areas.[5]

When curriculum specialists and 5Cs coaches engage in professional learning, the intended outcome is that 5Cs coaches will take what they learn and work with teachers in their school sites in ways they and their principals and professional learning teams find to be most effective. Coaches and their sites are required to focus professional learning on what Fujimoto and her team have determined is the strategic direction for the year, but the ways in which they roll it out and the methods they choose are at the discretion of the site. Professional learning in support of the Capstone is an example of how this part of the system works.

As we have mentioned previously, all school sites were expected to have designed a Capstone experience for their eighth- or twelfth-grade students by the end of the 2021–2022 academic year. The DO professional learning shop produced and disseminated documents that explained what the Capstone is intended to be and how to implement it. Implementation is anchored by the development of student portfolios that contain performance task assessments (PTAs) and student reflections. Additional artifacts may be included in the portfolio that comprises the student's "raw material" to prepare for the end-of-the-year Capstone experience.

Fujimoto and her team start from the principle that the Capstone is intended to reveal to the student, her teachers, and an adult panel her cognitive and affective growth in terms of technical skills, twenty-first-century skills, and youth voice and purpose. At its core, the Capstone is an exercise in metacognition for the student and assessment for the educators who help create the experience. To help teachers make the Capstone meaningful for students, Fujimoto focused the curriculum specialists and 5Cs coaches on the PTAs because of their importance as building blocks for the portfolio and the Capstone project. She and the curriculum specialists designed an experience in which the 5Cs coaches adopted the role of teachers engaged in professional learning so they would understand firsthand the structure, process, and outcomes of the professional learning they would provide at their sites. At the end, they reflected on their own application of the 5Cs as they moved through the session. Integrating the 5Cs with content learning is at the core of a meaningful PTA; thus, it was vital for the coaches to experience what that feels like and what they learned from it so they could effectively work with teachers at their sites.

The method the DO professional learning shop uses has four major components: (1) a focus on the most important instructional objectives for the year, (2) experiential professional learning in which participants follow the same path teachers and students are expected to follow in classrooms, (3) reflection on one's own learning, and (4) extending the learning to other teachers. Fujimoto and the curriculum specialists are intentionally modeling focus, experience, reflection, and application ("Our modeling is essential") because these are the methods that they want employed at school sites. It is probably obvious by now, but this is the opposite of the "sit-and-get" professional development sessions teachers have detested for decades. Prepared in this way, 5Cs coaches help teachers design PTAs reflective of their understanding of students' strengths and needs.

Curriculum specialists also provide professional learning for other cohorts of teachers, including department chairs and school site teacher leaders for programs such as AIME, Democracy Schools, and Community Schools. They employ similar methods for all these cohorts. Fujimoto's ambition is to make professional learning as coherent as possible so that teacher leaders in a wide range of positions across the district and administrators are speaking with one voice about how to progress toward CPSF goals.

Professional Learning Through Program Implementation

Teachers lead the implementation of new programs that support the CPSF to the greatest extent possible because when they have opportunities to innovate and be creative (autonomy and choice), they are more deeply committed to the program and more inclined to persuade other teachers to adopt the innovation. Initiatives that reach into classrooms require learning on two levels—content and pedagogy. Thus, teachers engaged in starting something new enhance their pedagogical content knowledge through job-embedded professional learning. We illustrate this work with two examples, Community Schools, and CTE pathways.

COMMUNITY SCHOOLS. AUHSD's approach to professional learning has evolved alongside the resurgence in the concept of Community Schools. Increasing inequality, gaps in delivery of health care and social services, lack of affordable housing, social and environmental justice issues, rising crime rates, and access to meaningful jobs have triggered unprecedented interest in Community Schools. The concept is decades old, simple to understand, and challenging to implement. Community Schools respond to gaps in resources and opportunities we have named by bringing health care, a social safety net, and other resources into school sites to create easier access for students and their families. AUHSD's ambition to create pathways to and from community resources available to students makes Community Schools an ideal tactic for achieving CPSF goals. To prevent Community Schools implementation from being on campus but not part of students' educational experiences, AUHSD determined to weave them into school life with explicit curriculum and pedagogy aligned with the CPSF.

Community Schools represent an important opportunity for reforms that focus on the whole student, providing access to social capital, and elevating youth voice and purpose. According to the Learning Policy Institute, "Community schools represent a place-based strategy in which schools partner with community agencies and allocate resources to provide an integrated focus on academics, health, and social services, youth and community development, and community engagement."[6]

New positions are required to take advantage of community resources present in the school not only to support students' basic needs but to enhance their learning. Under the guidance of Community Schools director Carlos Hernandez, AUHSD has created a teacher lead position at each of the district's thirteen Community Schools. Their purpose is to work with teacher colleagues to design learning experiences that integrate community issues such as access to health care, affordable housing, healthy food availability, and other pressing issues in the community. Opportunities are available through other CPSF programs such as the CTE Patient Care pathway and the Magnolia Agriscience Community Center. The challenge is to link classroom- and school-based programs with new opportunities available via Community Schools. Teacher leads get support from the DO professional learning shop to figure out the curriculum and pedagogical tactics needed to integrate Community Schools with other learning opportunities and curricula in a wide range of teachers' classrooms. Their involvement in Community Schools broadens and deepens their understanding of new approaches to teaching and learning as they bring colleagues along.

Returning to Elmore, we can see that the implications are clear: integrating Community Schools services with students' educational experiences is a new demand on the system. AUHSD is addressing the systemic need by adding the teacher lead and a classified staff position that supports Community Schools operations. Coming from the general faculty, teacher leads must expand their skills and knowledge to perform well in a complicated, nonclassroom role. They serve as vital trim tabs as they lead other teachers to integrate community issues such as food deserts, environmental justice, and homelessness (to name a few) into classroom teaching. Professional learning is already focused on the 5Cs and implementing the Capstone project. AUHSD supports teacher leads by helping them also learn how tactics that support CPSF goals can be applied to enrich students' educational experiences in the Community Schools context. Jemma Rodriguez, teacher lead at Sycamore Junior High School, expresses the enthusiasm that comes from being empowered to discover new ways of working with students:

> Through the Community School strategy, we are taking care of the whole child. For instance, a single student has received on-site services such as mental health counseling, holiday and winter clothing sponsorship through the school's "Angel Tree," and conflict mediation through *restorative justice practices within the classroom*. The same student's family has also been referred to the resource center where they have received guidance and resource connections for legal matters and other basic needs, such as food and school uniforms.[7]

Rodriguez's reflection indicates that many educators are learning by doing as they address the needs of the whole student. They apply their skills and knowledge to solve problems and enrich students' lives. It is also true that collective teacher learning takes place with projects such as Community Schools as explained by Grant Shuster, president of the teacher association in AUHSD:

> Through the practices of shared leadership, engaging the community, providing integrated student supports, and enriching student learning inside and outside of the classroom, we are focused to ensure the whole child and their family are supported to thrive. This process has more potential to transform public education than anything I have seen in my 30 years of teaching.[8]

Figure 6.1 is a representation of Community Schools as a reimagined schoolhouse that aligns closely with AUHSD's ambitions to create synergy between the schools and the community. It symbolizes three-level chess on behalf of students and suggests how much educators need to learn to make it run well.

CAREER AND TECHNICAL EDUCATION PATHWAYS. Table 4.2 lists all the CTE pathways currently operating in AUHSD. Many are new and have teacher cham-

FIGURE 6.1 *Community Schools as the schoolhouse of the future*

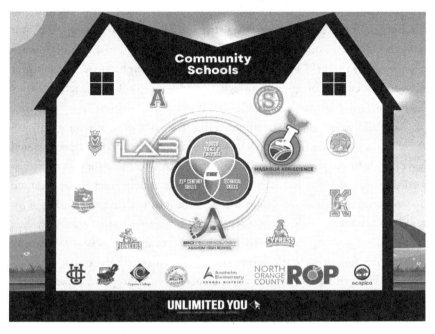

pions who had to expand their content knowledge and pedagogy into novel fields. They did so with help from university and private enterprise partners available through the network described in chapter 4. The vast majority of the pathways listed have content outside of what most teacher education programs would provide as content concentrations. Cybersecurity, Biotechnology, and Drone Technology would align with teachers of computer science, biology, and physics, but teachers graduating from credentialing programs and relevant majors would not necessarily have the application knowledge required to teach the pathway. The State of California requires work experience as part of teacher certification to be eligible to teach in a CTE pathway. Thus, professional learning consists of expanding teacher knowledge of how to apply academic content to jobs and figuring out experience-based pedagogy required for students' hands-on learning in CTE. Through this learning, teachers expand the range of student experiences and, thus, opportunities for them to find purpose.

Professional learning for CTE teaching is unusual in that much of it takes place in isolation—an individual teacher figuring out how to teach new content in new ways. AUHSD strives to break down this isolation informally and formally. The district matched two teachers to lead the development and teaching of cybersecurity. One has a strong track record teaching CTE, but not cybersecurity, at the junior high school level. (He had to accumulate work experience in the field to get certified.) The other taught at the same junior high with a career background in cybersecurity, but no CTE teaching. They both transferred to Magnolia High School to start the cybersecurity pathway.

AUHSD uses federal Vocational Education Act money (commonly referred to as Carl Perkins money) to support teachers' individual professional learning. It funds participation in various workshops, including monthly advisory board meetings for each CTE pathway that help teachers understand how to build courses so they align with specific jobs and careers. The larger intent is to keep teachers in contact with industry experts so that their curricula and pedagogy are up to date. The district has set up a professional learning community format so that teachers from each pathway have ample opportunities to learn from one another and partners from appropriate sectors in the economy. AUHSD continually works to strengthen the ties among teachers, classrooms, and the world of work.

Exiting the Egg Crate with AIME Partners

Teachers usually teach side by side in classrooms that are largely isolated, in what resembles an egg crate. Classrooms are walled off from each other and from the world beyond the school, even with contemporary uses of technology. Current practices are beginning to break that down, but for AUHSD teachers to open their classrooms to the outside world, they need to understand that world better. AUHSD is piloting an externship experience for teachers in which volunteers can spend time in and learn from a for-profit or nonprofit enterprise in the community.

> The AIME Teacher Externship is designed to get teachers out of the classroom and into the workplace so that they can see the career readiness skills that students need and make them more real in the classroom for their students.
> —SCOTT REINDL, COORDINATOR, 21ST CENTURY CAREER READINESS[9]

As a deeply committed partner, Tim Nguyen invited a group of teachers to learn how a nonprofit such as MeridianLink operates. The goal was to help teachers understand the professional expectations in such a company so that they could teach content and the 5Cs in ways that were authentic for the world of work. The plan so far is for teachers to visit work sites and shadow individuals to learn more about the daily needs of a professional workplace.

> As a teacher, you're always asking yourself, "Am I preparing my kids for . . . not just for college, but also careers?" Here at EK headquarters, it's just so awesome to work with the professionals here and think about my own classroom and see if there is a parallel between what's happening in the workforce and what is happening in my classrooms.
> —DR. JEFF KIM, SOUTH JUNIOR HIGH SCHOOL HISTORY TEACHER

> One overarching theme is the necessity of . . . those soft skills that we incorporate with the technical skills.
> —JASON COLLAR, SOUTH JUNIOR HIGH SCHOOL HISTORY TEACHER

> There are project management tools that I am eager to bring back to the classrooms.
> —CHRISTIE NARANJO, ANAHEIM HIGH SCHOOL ENGLISH TEACHER

Grassroots Professional Learning

AUHSD has a history of embracing innovation from the classroom with subsequent adoption within and across schools that predates Matsuda's superintendency. The origins of the Capstone project are one such example.[10] Another prominent example is the Writing Journey, the brainchild of longtime (now retired) AUHSD English language arts teacher Kelly Gallagher.[11] Different from previous efforts to achieve writing across the curriculum, the Writing Journey sought to expand what teachers perceived as worthwhile writing and to demonstrate how writing enhances learning within all content areas.

Gallagher used his experience as one of the first curriculum specialists and his understanding of how the school district worked as a system to generate interest in and support for the Writing Journey prior to any launch. He enlisted the support of leadership first with research-informed arguments about the importance of persuasive writing in students' development. He advocated for the importance of student voice long before the centrality of the concept in the CPSF. With leadership endorsement, Gallagher presented his thinking to a captive audience of all the district's teachers to make his case and provide food for thought. Leadership created a position of teacher on special assignment exclusively for him in which he continued to teach two classes and had the rest of his time to follow up on his initial presentation with teachers across the district.

In the first year, Gallagher met with teachers in all departments at the district's high schools during their late-start professional learning time. As a peer with a deep understanding of the opportunities in classrooms and the burdens of reading and assessing student work, Gallagher facilitated teachers' design of writing in courses as disparate as chemistry and US history. Nothing was mandated. It was up to teachers to figure out assignments, sequence, timing, and so on, with Gallagher addressing specific questions about writing and the logistics of embedding it into instruction.

At the beginning of year two, Gallagher once again had all the district's teachers as his audience. This time, however, he asked teachers who had tried embedding more writing into their teaching to present their experiences. Thus, teachers heard how a math teacher adapted the social studies method of analyzing the news article of the week to having math students write about the *graph* of the week. And there were others. Gallagher's method was to share his experience and thinking to encourage other teachers to adopt essential principles into their own teaching and then demonstrate to their peers what they were able to do and why they believed it had value. In the process, teachers were elevated as creative professionals who knew how to enhance teaching and learning.

In subsequent years, Matsuda mandated that schools schedule at least one late start with Gallagher, which helped open the door to his work with departments. Gallagher began to use his classroom as a laboratory that bore some resemblance to Lesson Study.[12] Interested teachers met with him before his first class for a briefing on what he intended to do and then observed one or both of his subsequent classes. Observations were followed by discussion. This process aligns most closely with the DO professional learning shop. Teachers experienced Gallagher's teaching through observation and then followed up with a metacognitive conversation. This method could be easily employed by a 5Cs coach, department chair, or any other teacher leader.

Gallagher also worked with school site administrations that expressed interest. When Savanna High School developed the first Capstone, the Writing Journey was an ideal fit because, when done right, it included students' unique voices and reflections on their learning across the curriculum. Post-COVID, the Writing Journey has since faded as a specific program, but its instructional strategy lives on in PTAs, portfolios, and the Capstone. Equally important, Gallagher's method is widely viewed as a strong example of the kind of teacher leadership AUHSD seeks to foster.

Summary

AUHSD sustains several avenues for teacher professional learning and growth. These investments in educators are essential to meet the needs of teachers working hard every day to improve students' educational experiences. Integrating twenty-first-century skills with technical skills in a manner that elevates youth voice and purpose is not something most AUHSD teachers were educated to do when they started teaching. They need opportunities to shift their mind-sets about their role and to develop new capacities. As extensive as professional learning in AUHSD is, district leaders, principals, and teacher leaders know that there is no straight, upward-sloping growth line for teachers either individually or collectively. Professional learning practices are challenged by human motivation.

> *Food for Thought 6.2*
> What are the greatest professional learning needs in your school or district? How consistent is professional learning *method* with professional learning *content*? Do multiple pathways exist to meet different needs?

THE FOUR-ROOM APARTMENT

In chapter 2, we discussed resistance to change in a general way using Lewin's concepts of freezing, unfreezing, and refreezing. Here we examine resistance to change at the individual level to look into teacher's motivation to change or not and think about what leaders and others can do with this motivation so that professional learning is most effective.

The Four-Room Apartment provides an explanation that demonstrates ways in which achieving ambitious reform such as the CPSF can falter.[13] Figure

6.2 is our graphic representation of the Four-Room Apartment. The bars between rooms represent hallways in the apartment. Note that there is no direct hallway leading to the Renewal Room. The only way to get there is through the Confusion Room.

People find themselves in different rooms for various reasons. Leaders seeking change try to recognize who is in which room and why, because their job during improvement efforts is to move people out of complacency or denial into and through confusion to achieve renewal. We examine each room and its occupants' needs in some detail.

Complacency

Those who are complacent generally feel good about the status quo. It works for them. Their tagline is likely, "If it ain't broke, don't fix it." What they do not recognize is that the status quo actually runs counter to stated goals and does not work for many people who are outside their attention. To help occupants feel less complacent requires bringing them into creative tension. Until they recognize the distance between their everyday reality and the vision for where their school is headed, they are unlikely to attempt change. Leaders use evidence—quantitative and qualitative data—to make their case

FIGURE 6.2 *The (modified) Four-Room Apartment*

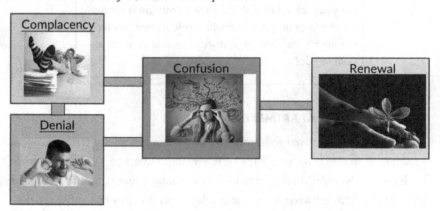

Source: Adapted from Marvin R. Weisbord, *Productive Workplaces Revisited: Dignity, Meaning, and Community in the 21st Century* (San Francisco: Jossey-Bass, 2004), 335.

for creative tension. They may also enlist help from teacher colleagues who already understand current needs and are waiting for others to join them in the Confusion Room.

Denial

As the name and the image suggest, the person in the Denial Room doesn't want to hear or see problems outside their room. This person may in fact be unhappy with the status quo but would rather not deal with it. Thus, the more comfortable path is to deny the problems that exist. This person is likely to seek protection through undiscussables. We encountered a recent example with a teacher who refused to let their student miss a day of class to contribute to a schoolwide program. The teacher's rationale was that the student was behind and could not afford to miss even one class. The teacher appears to have denied two things: (1) that the student's desire to be part of a schoolwide effort was a good sign about their affiliation with the school, and (2) the teacher had a role they were playing in the student's low performance. These two issues and more were not on the table for discussion, and the teacher simply refused to approve the student to miss class for a school-sponsored program. Occupants of the Denial Room also need to encounter creative tension, but it may not happen until the strongest undiscussables are opened up and worked through.

Confusion

In this room, learning happens, but it is hard. We need to let go of old ideas that might have helped us be complacent or in denial and try to find new ideas that will improve what we are doing. The process of moving from old to new is confusing, as we try new techniques or strategies that do not work well at first. Implementation dips, as described by Fullan, are rife in the Confusion Room, as some educators attempt to improve, others hold back, and some constantly criticize.[14]

Teacher leaders, principals, and district office administrators have different and important roles to play with respect to the Confusion Room. Teachers and principals striving for change work to clarify what is confusing and simultaneously tamp down anxiety about making change. This subtle leadership both supports and prods. The leader's goal is to move people through the Confusion Room as quickly as possible while not motivating a retreat back to complacency or denial. Meanwhile, district-level leaders can help by metaphorically standing in the hallways with the message, "There is no going back. You need to keep moving toward our future." It takes a great deal of resolve to work in and keep people moving through the Confusion Room.

Renewal

Renewal is where change is allowed to flourish, such as a school district that has transformed from test-based college preparation to educating for purposeful life. Moving from confusion to renewal is professionally gratifying and beneficial for the intended audience: high school graduates in the case of the CPSF. True renewal is a process that needs constant nurturing. Leadership turnover, local emergencies, and changing state and federal policies can allow for or motivate retreat back into the Confusion, Denial, and Complacency Rooms. It happens all too often.

Dynamics

People can enter the Renewal Room only by moving through the Confusion Room. This is the central challenge of changing the status quo. As Lewin suggested, people may change their minds when presented with evidence of a need to change or the benefits from change, but he does not clarify the role of leaders. Education leaders are likely to be those who present evidence to multiple constituents—from teachers to board members and community members. Their job as change agents is to support these constituents as they move into the Confusion Room and grapple with difficult learning. There are dangers here. The unpleasantness of the Confusion Room can easily generate internal political trends that, if left unchecked, will make martyrs of leaders. Realistically, not everyone will make it to the Renewal Room, but a critical mass helps change the status quo for the interlocking systems we have described. Those who remain in complacency and denial cannot be ignored, even if we would like to do so, because their negative communications will fester and undermine renewal. They require more time and attention to move through their confusion and join successful educators in the Renewal Room.

> *Food for Thought 6.3*
>
> When faced with the prospect of change, which room do you run to out of habit? How is this similar to or different from people with whom you work? What motivates you into the Confusion Room, if anything?

CONCLUSION

Professional learning is multifaceted, reaching different teachers in different ways. Successful professional learning will take advantage of existing systems and create new ones to stimulate teacher learning and improvement in ways consistent with the district's vision, mission, and goals. It is important to remember that, just as with students, professional learning cannot be exclusively cognitive. Teachers have feelings, too, and those feelings motivate them to back the status quo, sometimes in perverse ways. Administrators and teacher leaders can use the Four-Room Apartment as a way to understand teacher resistance and how they might address it. A learning organization motivates and supports people to move through the Four-Room Apartment toward renewal. Doing so is vital to changing educational experiences in classrooms and, by extension, the nature of secondary education.

TAKING STOCK

All too often, professional learning sessions are at the top of the list of gatherings teachers love to hate. We believe that Diana Fujimoto and her team have figured out ways to circumvent teachers' distaste for professional learning by engaging them in experiential learning. Despite the high quality of such experiences, resisters are ever-present. The following questions we pose are intended to help you reflect on the nature and quality of professional learning in your district and your own general perspective about change:

1. If you are an administrator, do you attend teacher professional learning sessions from start to finish?
   - How does the experience strike you as an educator? Are you generally engaged or bored? Do you believe that you learn something new when you participate?
   - If you do not attend, why not? How will you know the effectiveness of what you and others put in front of teachers?
2. Does your district have a theory of action that permeates all teacher professional learning provided to teachers?
   - Is your district's professional learning consistently aligned with district vision, mission, and goals?
   - In what ways are school site and DO administrators involved in professional learning?
3. Think of a recent change that was announced in your district. What room did you occupy after you were informed? Was there anything that motivated you into the Confusion Room? Did you make it to renewal?

CHAPTER 7

THE PROMISE OF THE CAREER PREPAREDNESS SYSTEMS FRAMEWORK

> The more students work at storing the deposits entrusted to them, the less they develop the critical consciousness which would result from their intervention in the world as transformers of that world.
>
> —PAOLO FREIRE[1]

THROUGHOUT THIS BOOK, we have asserted that for young people, particularly marginalized portions of the secondary school population, achieving the American Dream through public school as we have known it is out of reach. It may never have been within reach for the majority of low-income, immigrant students. Philip Schlechty said it best at a professional development workshop one of us attended in the 1990s: "We're doing a better job than ever of educating students for the 1950s."[2] We hope that by the time you read this final chapter, we have convinced you that contemporary education that would be familiar to 1950s graduates is unacceptable. A dramatic redirection of US education is both urgent and important. The CPSF is not a quick fix for an inadequate status quo. It is a vision for a permanently changed future.

THE FUTURE OUR CHILDREN NEED

Implementation of the CPSF and aligned reforms creates a new culture of shared learning and cocreation of educational experiences that address the whole adolescent student—head and heart; identity and aspiration; work and family; neighborhood and community. Students educated in this way find and raise their voice, move forward toward their purpose, their calling. They are set on a path toward self-actualization and self-transcendence. These lofty and vital goals of the CPSF challenge educators to achieve their reasons for entering education in the first place, to work toward personal mastery and to be the kinds of teachers who are valued and remembered for a lifetime.

Readers could be thinking, "That works for them in AUHSD, but could never work here because . . ." and they might fill in the blank with any number of reasons. Chief among them are likely to be resources and community partners. These are indeed major challenges. What we have found in AUHSD, however, is that when school districts seek grants for creative ideas, they are able to find funding; when educators reach out, the community reaches back. Partnering in the ways we have described throughout the book is attractive to higher education institutions, private enterprise, and local government because all are strengthened in the process. Jobs for graduates mean motivated employees. Civic engagement leads to municipalities that are communities and to civic pride among citizens. We have found that, as demanding as getting projects and programs started in AUHSD has been, once initiated, partners *seek out the district* because they want to be involved. Former Anaheim mayor Tom Tait led the way toward civic engagement. The Kaiser hospital system provided the first AIME internships. They stand as shining examples to other community organizations eager to engage with AUHSD. Grant funders often reach out to the district now because they are looking for impactful programs to support. Most partners and funders are attracted to the district as a beacon of effective innovation in the name of student success.

Googling AUHSD

In March 2021, Matsuda was approached by Lisa Gevelber, the Google executive who founded and leads Grow with Google, the company's $100 million initiative to make Google Career Certificates available to 20,000 job seekers. Google predicts that the job acquisition potential of the certificates will generate $1 billion in new wages.[3] Gevelber and her team had identified AUHSD as an urban district leading workforce development through dual enrollment, CTE pathways, AIME, and the constant cultivation of student voice and purpose. In their discussions, Gevelber pointed out that jobs today require some level of digital skills in a country where more than 65 percent of the population does not have a college degree. She sought a partnership that would add Google Career Certificates to the range of workplace opportunities available to AUHSD students. Having proved the concept of the certificates as an avenue to jobs (over 300,000 globally), Gevelber's idea was to embed certificate education into existing AUHSD courses. Doing so would give students free access to technical skills development in areas such as information technology, data analytics, and project management—certificated skills that could be put to use in well-paying jobs immediately after high school graduation. Part-time work might support college education, or students might use their certificates for sought-after internships during full-time college attendance. The certificate program opens a new door for student purpose and supports the district's vision, mission, and core values. Furthermore, certificates provide a practical means of narrowing the equity gap that low-income, immigrant, and otherwise marginalized students face throughout the United States.

AUHSD embraces the classroom and teacher leadership as levers—trim tabs—of positive change and implementation of CPSF programs. In the summer of 2021, more than twenty teachers took one Google Career Certificate course in information technology, data analytics, or project management. Of these, about a dozen integrated what they learned into their high school curricula that ranged across computer science, biotechnology, ethnic studies, English, and yearbook. These teachers were encouraged to take risks and to innovate within a broad circle of autonomy and choice. What these teachers learned individually could lead to organizational learning that leverages practical skills development to achieve the ideal of educating for purposeful life. Consistent with a learning organization, the district encourages teachers to take risks and learn from successes and mistakes with initiatives such Google Career Certificates.

By May of 2021, over 150 students successfully completed a certificate. As of this writing, the number of teachers offering embedded certificates has grown, and approximately 850 students are expected to earn at least one certificate by the end of the 2022–2023 academic year. Adding Google Career Certificates to the range of career-readiness offerings shows great promise. Students in courses with integrated certificate education are experiencing learning differently and are thinking more strategically about how to apply their learning in the twenty-first-century world of work, career, and adulthood. AUHSD classrooms are leaving the 1950s behind.

Envisioning the Future

We have a colleague who uses the metaphor of flaws in the educational system becoming "part of the wallpaper."[4] They are so much a part of life in schools, they're not even noticed by educators or the community. AUHSD has adopted a systemic approach to criticizing what would otherwise go unnoticed in the wallpaper and addressing long-standing defects in educational theories of action. The district has taken particular aim at a standards and testing regime run amok. Transformative experiences of the type long ago imagined by Dewey and his band of Progressives are not confined to a single classroom, school, or a small group of zealous teachers. The wide aperture through which all the district's students see opportunities to give their current and future lives purpose is available in all the district's schools and classrooms. Institutionally, the district administration, school board, higher education community, and local nonprofit partners within the Anaheim Educational Collaborative have embraced the mission to keep that aperture open and the opportunities within reach. The collaborative is one of the many mechanisms that ensures the future of educating for purposeful life in Anaheim.

The graduates represented in these pages have had their lives transformed by educational experiences not yet common in secondary schools. They identify attention to their affective development as crucial to their cognitive development and competence as they left high school and emerged into the worlds of work and higher education. Some are inspired to share their experiences and wisdom with the next generation.

If AUHSD is able to achieve its vision for all students, then it may be true that parents' dreams and visions are achieved as well. All parents want the best for their children. All parents want their children to succeed in ways they had never imagined for themselves. Participation in Community Schools, learning from students about their experiences, and seeing their own place in their children's development help parents to achieve their purpose alongside their children. By understanding the importance of family assets, the district enlists parents in the education of their children through guided tours of classrooms in which teaching and learning are taking place, through parent education programs, and in the future, through Google Career Certificates offered to parents. Supporting families strengthens kids.

We do not claim that every experience is unique to AUHSD or that we reach every student to the same degree. What we do claim, however, is that the district is on an upward trajectory toward educating for purposeful life such that, one day, every student will graduate having figured out the adult they wish to become and acquired the skills and knowledge they need to take them there. When this vision is fully achieved, it will be the result of weaving together what works, what is new, and what is needed in a manner that takes advantage of multiple systems while understanding the interactions of those systems with the individuals who make them run.

> *Food for Thought 7.1*
> What sort of potential partners exist in your school district's community? Are there community colleges, retailers, ranchers, research facilities, manufacturing plants, social service agencies, farmers, nonprofits, and other service providers striving to strengthen your community? Are they committed to finding the next generation of innovators and leaders? In what ways does your student population align with philanthropic organizations committed to urban, suburban, or rural education?

STRATEGIC POSITIONING

Early in this book we acknowledged that, despite countless cycles of reform, little changes in education from year to year. We fully understand the vulnerability of ambitious education reform, and we worry that the CPSF could fade even before it is fully implemented. We recognize that implementation is never finished. Bringing reform into fruition requires patience and persistence. The CPSF is not a task to be completed. We recognize that internal and external politics are built into the very foundation of public schools, particularly large systems, and that multiple and competing interests must be managed through committed, interlocking coalitions. To both cynics and idealists, we say that school leaders and educators generally must be adaptable to local circumstances and unforeseen events as they stay focused on vision, mission, and values.

Responding to Uncertainty and Ambiguity

In the early 2000s, following the 9/11 terrorist attacks, the US Army War College's military planners were worried about the radically different international security environment. They found themselves at an inflection point in the aftermath of an extreme demonstration of asymmetrical power—three hijacked passenger aircraft punctured domestic security in the heart of the world's most powerful military. The entire military and intelligence apparatus was confronted with unprecedented uncertainty and ambiguity. The War College determined a need to understand the security environment as volatile, uncertain, complex, and ambiguous, or VUCA.[5] A VUCA perspective requires acknowledgment that old routines and beliefs may not fit the changing environment that is not fully understood at any given point of time. The War College needed greater flexibility and imagination in its thinking about and response to threats.

The COVID-19 pandemic presented education with the shock of the decade. A general preoccupation with "learning loss" suggests that we have seen an inflection point in education—one that points downward as we lament what students do not have. This point of view leads educators and policy makers into yearning for the "good old days" prepandemic when kids were in "normal" school and were progressing well. But "normal" and "progressing well" are part of a post-pandemic myth that everything was better before. It wasn't. In simple terms, the pandemic threw all educators into the Confusion Room of the Four-Room Apartment. They had a choice to either move through the Confusion Room to renewal or wait for the pandemic to pass so they could retreat into the Complacency and Denial Rooms. Most seem to have chosen retreat.

AUHSD, in contrast, has adopted a VUCA perspective to use the learning that takes place in the Confusion Room to keep moving toward renewal. The district is wary of threats, but also eager to find newly available resources to maintain and increase CPSF momentum. For example, the pandemic and its after-effects brought students' and families' physical and mental well-being to the forefront of Sacramento policy makers' attention. The result is billions of new dollars for Community Schools. AUHSD was poised to use these new dollars to expand the Community Schools already started under the CPSF and become one of three demonstration sites for the state. Understanding how quickly the political and fiscal environment can change—how volatile it is—and making the uncertain more certain allows AUHSD to flourish while other districts are stuck in a route that returns them to a status quo that was not doing that well in the first place. In the process, AHUSD has created its own inflection point coming out of the pandemic, one that trends upward.

What about complexity and ambiguity? Chapter 2 has numerous concepts that we have strived to put together in a framework precisely because educating secondary school students is a complex process. We want to demonstrate to readers that complexity requires individual and systemic intelligence that yields innovative and effective answers to problems that are not easily understood and solved. At the root of complexity is ambiguity—there is something in the district's organizational environment that cannot be readily understood through data collection, observation, or analysis. It must be experienced, reflected upon, experimented with, and learned from. That is the pattern for many, if not all, of the CPSF programs. How do we prepare students for work that has not yet been conceived? That question is addressed through external partnerships that bring expertise regarding present and future work into the district and classrooms. Outcomes cannot easily be predicted because, in an ambiguous world, they must be given time to emerge.

VUCA is a mind-set that embraces the reality that our ability to solve problems is limited by past experience and enhanced by experimentation, action, and systematic reflection. We find it hard to imagine the possibility of educating for purposeful life without embracing VUCA.

The Workforce Malaise

A surprising, little understood but much talked about after-effect of the pandemic seems to be reduced motivation to work. Quiet quitting has emerged as a post-pandemic workplace phenomenon. Zaid Khan, a Generation Z engineer, describes what this means: "I recently learned this term called quiet quitting, where you're not outright quitting on the job but you're quitting the idea of going above and beyond," Kahn says. "You're still performing your duties, but you're no longer subscribing to the hustle-culture mentality that work has to be your life. The reality is it's not. And your worth as a person is not defined by your labor."[6]

As of this writing, quiet quitting is trending as a phenomenon in the media. A recent Gallup poll finds that approximately half the US workforce is engaged in quiet quitting. Social media is rife with testimonials regarding this trend; people are doing the bare minimum to earn a paycheck. From this vantage point, there is a growing disassociation between employees and the enterprises in which they find work.[7]

Quiet quitting is a new name for a recurring malaise in the workplace. Dissatisfaction with work life has been documented from 1950s anonymous corporate America to 1960s dropouts to 1980s tech rebels introducing T-shirts, jeans, and flip-flops as statements of their independence, only to find that the perks of Ping-Pong and free food meant eighteen-hour or longer days at work and much less freedom than they had imagined. McGregor identified the problem in the 1950s and 1960s as a lack of motivation, specifically, no opportunity for self-actualization.[8] We agree with Kahn that work should not be a person's whole life. But we do not accept quiet quitting as just part of the wallpaper of work life. Quiet quitting—pretending to do one's job while really doing something else—is an indicator that the individual is marking time and collecting a paycheck, not aligning the It, We, and I of meaningful work. We believe that identifying a life purpose, maybe even several purposes, in adolescence draws youth into a calling. Working at a calling provides both a paycheck and personal fulfillment: meaningful work, self-actualization, and self-transcendence. It is the path toward a life well lived.

Unfortunately, schools in their current common form prepare students for quiet quitting because of their often stifling emphasis on compliance that teaches students to just get by. Contemporary educators will recognize their schools driven by compliance rules in Dewey's critique from the 1930s:

> Enforced quiet and acquiescence prevent pupils from disclosing their real natures. They enforce artificial uniformity. They put seeming before being. They place a premium on preserving the outward appearance of attention, decorum, and obedience. And everyone who is acquainted with schools in

which this system prevailed knows that thoughts, imaginations, desires, and sly activities ran their own unchecked course behind this façade.[9]

The familiar parable of the three bricklayers explains the difference between earning a paycheck and responding to a calling. Our version of this parable goes like this: After the Great Fire in London in 1666, the famous architect Christopher Wren was commissioned to rebuild St. Paul's Cathedral. One day he observed three bricklayers on a scaffold, one crouched, one half-standing, and one standing tall who was working very hard and fast. To the first bricklayer, Wren asked the question, "What are you doing?" to which the bricklayer replied, "I'm a bricklayer. I'm doing my job to feed my family." When asked the same question, the second bricklayer responded, "I'm doing my job so someday I can be manager of bricklayers. I want to be the boss." But the third bricklayer, the most productive of the three, said with pride, "I'm building a cathedral because it is my calling to serve God."

AUHSD educators aspire to help students find their calling and thereby joy in work. Workplace malaise is largely caused by a poor fit among the individual, the nature of the work, and the way the work is organized and incentivized. Education can do its part to help young people avoid what for them are mindless, unfulfilling jobs and the resulting poor performance and unhappiness by helping them find the cathedral they wish to help build, even if it means striking out on their own. To do so, schools must become places of self-discovery and external exploration.

We want AUHSD graduates to make informed decisions about what they most want to do once they graduate, and we do not judge those decisions. Students may choose to enter the military, go to community college, work in the tech industry, or build houses. The point is that they *choose* rather than enter a life predetermined by the systems in which they find themselves.

Martin Luther King Jr. wrote about this kind of choice: "If a man is 'called' to be a street sweeper, he should sweep streets even as Michelangelo painted, or Beethoven composed music, or Shakespeare wrote poetry. He should sweep streets so well that all the hosts of heaven and earth will pause to say, 'here lived a great street sweeper who did his job well.'"[10]

Rafael Muñoz has been an AUHSD custodian for over twenty years. He works in the district office building taking care of the exterior and interior offices and bathrooms. Every day in the morning, he can be seen working diligently, smiling, and acknowledging district employees with a wave of his hand. In different circumstances, through educational opportunities, would his fate have been altogether changed? Maybe instead he would be working at a desk inside one of the offices he cleans. One day Matsuda approached Muñoz and thanked him for always exhibiting a smile and positive demeanor. He asked Muñoz what drives him. Muñoz explained that he has two boys who graduated from the district's Savanna High School. One is now in medical school and the other is studying to be an engineer. He said he knows how hard all the educators work and that if he could just do his part, making sure the bathrooms and workspaces are clean, our jobs would be just a little easier, and that makes him happy. One might never have guessed that the big-box structure of the AUHSD district office could be Muñoz the custodian's cathedral. His calling as he defines it is to support the work of the educators inside and in all of the district's schools.

For the vast majority of teachers, teaching is a calling. Their cathedral is built from a commitment to the whole child and to develop, in turn, that child's calling. As with physical cathedrals, the work is very long term and there are many obstacles to overcome. For at least two decades, teachers have been commanded to raise test scores. Some became leaders who appeared effective at raising test scores and took over the role of coercing more teachers to follow in their footsteps. They and the policy makers they appeased encouraged two generations of bricklayers who, instead of building a cathedral, have built enclosures that wall off students' true potential. We seek to liberate students and teachers alike to unleash their mutually supporting potential to develop children who are compassionate, connected within a community, and self-actualized as they find their calling through which they will achieve purposeful life.

> ### Food for Thought 7.2
> Are your district's stated values consistent with how you educate children? Will students in your school system know what they aspire to accomplish in their adult lives and have the means to do so? What is the most important work you can do right now to build an educational cathedral?

LESSONS LEARNED

The CPSF journey has taught and continues to teach us many lessons about personal mastery and leading meaningful change. Probably the hardest lesson of all is accepting that change is a messy process. Feeling stuck in the Confusion Room easily causes panic, dread of a disappointing future, and lost sleep. Leaders need faith in themselves that they can clean up the messes that inevitably occur as long as they stay true to the kind of education they envision for all students. And no one travels alone.

Leadership Matters

A systems thinking perspective helps us to understand that there is great power in teachers, teacher leaders, administrators, board members, and community members committed to the vision—"To create a better world through Unlimited You"—with the understanding, tools, and guidance to play three-level chess. Few people come ready-made for this level of sophisticated professionalism. Dispositions such as ontological humility, working with creative tension, striving for personal mastery, and treating everyone with compassion require individual and collective development and constant nurturing. We have learned, and continue to learn, that falling back on bureaucratic rules, roles, and norms stifles sound decision-making and compromises systems thinking.

The quality of students' educational experiences is a collective effort easily undermined by just one teacher in their school day. Principals are the linchpins for creating strong schools that embrace the ambition of elevating youth voice and purpose. They can implement initiatives working with key teacher leaders and help them increase their influence through new and existing structures. Principals appoint department chairs, make committee assignments, help design master schedules, and collaborate to shape professional learning. They create the teacher corps at their schools through recruitment, hiring, evaluating, dismissing, and promoting teachers to tenured status. More subtly, principals need to recognize their trim tab teachers, both positive and negative, and find ways to empower the positive. These principals have integrity and the courage to be transparent when the school begins to lose its way, and they know when to celebrate the course corrections and thereby communicate on a daily basis what all of the educators in the building are working to achieve on behalf of students.

Principals and their teacher leaders cannot do this work effectively on their own. They need DO leaders who have the humility to listen first, then problem-solve *with*, instead of fix things *for*, the principal. The DO must stand with its principals in the mess, keeping their eye on the higher purpose and doing their part to clean up as the school moves forward. The superintendent must choose a cabinet and directors carefully to ensure that their daily work aligns with a compassionate, values-driven culture. It is the superintendent's job to guide these leaders so that there is coherence from the boardroom to the classroom.

Narrative Matters

Franklin D. Roosevelt was a master of narrative. Matsuda often refers to his metaphor of lending a hose to a neighbor whose house is burning to explain to the American public the importance of "lending" the United Kingdom and France old warships and supplies as their nations stood against the Nazis. Effective narratives work on many levels—personal, political, and practical. Those who have teamed up to make the CPSF a reality need to see themselves and their personal and professional purposes in the narrative.

When describing the CPSF to business partners, Matsuda explains that the district is striving to graduate future employees committed to the purpose of their enterprises and the community at large. When addressing civil rights and social justice advocates, he emphasizes the cultivation of student voice. For parents, the narrative is about helping their kids to stand on their own two feet while providing resources and support to their families. For teachers, the message is about the autonomy and choice they must exercise to educate the whole child and achieve their calling as educators.

The all-embracing narrative is that players at all three levels of chess are allies facing the most formidable foe in education—the status quo. The resistance to change from the status quo is fierce because change means that someone's world will be disrupted; people will feel that if one group of students is benefiting as never before, then those tied to the status quo will lose. The coalition of devoted educators and community members must counter with the narrative that the CPSF is for the good of all and does not play favorites depending on one group's power and status.

Politics Matter

Public schools are governed by elected boards. They hire the superintendent to keep them informed about school district operations, advise them regarding policy and procedure, and implement board policies reflective of their aspirations and, by extension, their constituents' aspirations for education in the district. School boards are often a focal point for local politics, and those politics are hotter than ever as a reflection of no-holds-barred conflict at the state and federal levels. Educators often wish to see themselves as separate from politics or apolitical, but three-level chess is, in many ways, a political game.

District leaders, especially superintendents, must know how to play on the third level of the chessboard. Doing so requires a realistic grasp of the political drivers and mental models influencing individual and collective school board decisions. Superintendent and cabinet success depends on robust relational capital with individual board members and the board as a whole. A major transformational construct such as the CPSF and the change it requires needs board commitment and support to allow district leaders to move forward under the criticism that will surely follow their change moves. Communication is key. Public figures are at their worst when surprised because they do not know how to react in the moment and are ever mindful of their public image. Keeping everyone moving in the same direction requires moving at a pace the board can understand and endorse. Getting too far out in front of the board can cause whiplash if board members believe they are losing support from the families they serve. Strong board relations help to manage community politics that allows for change.

District partners are cultivated constituents who can have great influence on school boards and thus district policy and external communications. If Kaiser Permanente, the City of Anaheim, and Loki.ai are cheerleaders for CTE pathways and AIME, then they reinforce board commitment to those programs and the CPSF generally. When the big voices in the community claim that the 5Cs are important to student development, board members and families are likely to listen. In the process, community partners help to inoculate the board and district administration from attacks motivated by trying to maintain the status quo or generate negative change.

In many states, unions are important political players. That is certainly the case in California. Unions can upend reform efforts that are seen as exploiting teachers or moving too fast for the profession. AUHSD has enlisted its local teacher association as an ally in the CPSF. Although this is a tricky maneuver, no teacher association can argue with teacher empowerment that encourages innovation and creativity to educate the whole student. It would be politically impossible for it to do so.

Voice Matters

Elevating student voice in the classroom and the community is a sea change in response to Dewey's critique about student docility and compliance in schools. Change in a system is, by definition, a disruption. When teachers and principals are expected to be at the forefront of creating changes that elevate student voice, they want their voices heard too. The systems, structures, and mind-sets described in this book are intended to provide places for ideas to be vetted and improved and educators to work as colleagues to solve instructional puzzles. The different voices of those striving to make the CPSF real are heard in the process of moving forward together. Metaphorically, their voices are the loudest in the Confusion Room, where the release of emotional tension is accepted as part of the process of unfreezing and moving to a better model for educating adolescents. Teacher voices and the wisdom that comes from them helps build momentum as they bring colleagues through the Confusion Room into renewal. Coherence is strengthened in the process. Elevating teacher voice reinforces the values AUHSD strives to put into practice with students. In other words, if the 5Cs are healthy for kids, they are good for adults too.

Patience Matters

A Chinese bamboo tree requires five years of watering and fertilizing before it will break through the ground. It requires patience to be rewarded with a five-year-old seedling that grows ninety feet in five weeks. The CPSF did not sprout from the district office fully formed. We would not want inspired readers to think they must wait five years to see growth, but we do advocate for patience with the mess, confusion, and missteps inevitable when creating positive change. The vision is achieved one step, one program at a time. Be patient, but not complacent. Change comes to fruition only when the whole system and all its subsystems are in place and fully functional. We believe that a minimum of three years is required to build cohesive systems and structures;

align vision, mission, and values within those systems and structures; become adept at three-level chess; and develop the habits of mind necessary to implement an education that leads students toward purposeful life.

FINAL THOUGHTS

We have done our best to be honest with our readers and to explain as clearly as we can how to frame education reform that makes a difference, what that reform yields, and the work yet to be done. We wish you well in your quest to change the educational experience for your students. You have to do the work, but you do not have to do it alone. We and others in our network stand ready as thought partners to help any way we can. The stakes are high, but together we can transform America by transforming our schools and educating all students for purposeful life.

TAKING STOCK

We end with a cluster of questions we intend to be provocative:

1. Would your mother feel right at home in your secondary schools? Would Harry Truman?
2. Is it acceptable to you that students would graduate from your high schools with little idea about what follows graduation for them?
3. When is the "right" time to transform education?
4. What will be your rallying cry, your call to action?
5. What three actions will you take this week to begin the process of improving students' educational experiences and prospects for a fulfilling life?

APPENDIX A

ADDITIONAL SOURCES OF SUPPORT FOR THE CPSF

There are many more programs and resources that support the CPSF than we have been able to discuss in this book. For anyone interested in learning more, we provide the following brief descriptions of a few of the important supports for the CPSF. We provide QR codes and web addresses with each description so you can access information easily.

Career Preparedness Systems Framework Whitepaper: This document is a brief, easily understood description of the CPSF. It may be a useful reference for understanding why the CPSF is important, what it is, how it is implemented, and how to get started educating for purposeful life in your own school district. https://drive.google.com/file/d/1FSR9Q2YDiUTep9l5K8gDo_UO95UEZ_Vs/view?usp=share_link.

Inflexion: Inflexion is a nonprofit partner that works with AUHSD in support of the CPSF. It is ready to support other school districts interested in educating for purposeful life through its Portico coaching program, support with action research, and other services. inflexion.org.

eKadence: This nonprofit was started with the mission of bringing an innovative, flexible, customizable learning management system to school districts at low or no cost. eKadence has partnered with AUHSD to find innovative ways to collect and analyze evidence of progress toward CPSF goals and the AUHSD vision. ekadence.org.

5Cs Rubric: Integrating the 5Cs into classroom instruction is fundamental to educating the whole child. Assessing students' skill development for twenty-first-century skills such as the 5Cs can be challenging. AUHSD has developed a rubric that captures students' skill development progress. https://drive.google.com/file/d/1-_wJXorMEaruvn4fDX2TVID0cseOgfBB/view?usp=share_link.

Capstone Playbook: AUHSD developed the playbook to help teachers and school site leaders plan students' progression toward meaningful Capstone experiences. The playbook has been an essential tool for implementing the Capstone at all the district's schools. https://drive.google.com/file/d/1YAjbylpU3qo40BhhCVW0c63tzWZSKpZE/view?usp=share_link.

TeachFX: This automated feedback tool provides quantitative and qualitative feedback to teachers that describes the frequency and nature of student voice in the classroom. teachfx.com.

Interview with Michael Fullan: With his vast experience in educational change, Michael Fullan has taken great interest in AUHSD. Superintendent Matsuda interviewed him for one of his Future Talks to discuss what is needed in US education today. https://www.youtube.com/watch?v=BgDE_9Y5BiY.

APPENDIX B

PROGRAMS THAT SUPPORT THE CPSF

Numerous programs and initiatives comprise the Career Preparedness Systems Framework. Throughout the book we have referenced signature programs that we consider clear illustrations of changed instructional design and how they were developed. In this appendix, we list them again and add more we believe readers will find informative. The AUHSD website (auhsd.us) is another great place to learn about programs that support the CPSF.

AIME Program: Anaheim's Innovative Mentoring Experience involves thousands of students in mentoring and internships with over ninety-five business and nonprofit partners. The summer internship program additionally provides a stipend, bus passes, and uniforms for students.

Anaheim Educational Collaborative: This consortium of higher education, elementary, nonprofit, and municipal representatives meets monthly with district leaders to design, implement, and monitor more cohesive alignment among K–16 educational institutions. The collaborative committed to the Anaheim Educational Pledge to better serve and prepare students for college and careers.

Democracy Schools: A civic-engagement program based on a model from the Mikva Foundation.[1] California offers a seal of civic engagement to recognized Democracy Schools educational experiences.

GEAR UP grant: A federal program, Gaining Early Awareness and Readiness for Undergraduate Programs, provides six- or seven-year grants to states and partnerships to provide services to high-poverty middle and high schools. GEAR UP grantees serve an entire cohort of students beginning no later than seventh grade and follow them through high school graduation. GEAR UP funds are also used to provide college scholarships to low-income students. AUHSD uses GEAR UP funds to support AIME, Magnolia Agriscience Community Center (MACC), summer enrichment, and other programs.

iLab: Incubate Learning, Accelerate Breakthroughs is located at Western High School and is open to students from across the district. Projects have included marketing initiatives for the MACC farm, biotech, and district-wide initiatives. The iLab partners with Empowered, a nonprofit organization based in Wichita, Kansas.

MACC: Students work on a farm located at Magnolia High School and use their learning for civic engagement. Projects have included addressing food deserts, obesity, and general health care.

NOTES

FOREWORD

1. Our team consists of Bill Hogarth, Joanne Quinn, Mag Gardner, Max Drummy, Jean Clinton, Bailey Fullan, Mary Jean Gallagher, and Santiago Rincon-Gallardo. See also Bailey Fullan and Joanne Quinn, *The Drivers* (Thousand Oaks, CA: Corwin, 2023), where we present a vignette case study of AUHSD, along with several other cases of new success from around the world.

INTRODUCTION

1. Ben Hurley, "The Fading American Dream in Numbers, and What You Can Do About It," Sustainability Harvard, 2022, https://www.top1000funds.com/2022/10/the-fading-american-dream-in-numbers-and-what-organisations-can-do-about-i/.
2. See Richard F. Elmore, *School Reform from the Inside Out: Policy, Practice, and Performance* (Cambridge, MA: Harvard Education Press, 2004); and Elizabeth A. City et al., *Instructional Rounds in Education: A Network Approach to Improving Teaching and Learning* (Cambridge, MA: Harvard Education Press, 2009).

CHAPTER 1

1. Robert P. Moses, "Speech on Freedom Summer at Stanford University" (speech, Palo Alto, CA, April 24, 1964), American Radio Works, https://americanradioworks.publicradio.org/features/blackspeech/bmoses.html.
2. Larry Cuban, *Confessions of a School Reformer* (Cambridge, MA: Harvard Education Press, 2021), xiv.
3. See, for example, Larry Cuban, *How Teachers Taught: Constancy and Change in American Classrooms 1880–1990,* 2nd ed. (New York: Teachers College Press, 1993); and Larry Cuban, *The Flight of a Butterfly or the Path of a Bullet? Using Technology to Transform Teaching and Learning* (Cambridge, MA: Harvard Education Press, 2018).
4. Anthony P. Carnevale, Artem Gulish, and Catherine P. Campbell, *If Not Now, When—An Urgent Need for an All-One-Systems Approach to Youth Policy* (Georgetown University: McCourt School of Public Policy, 2021).
5. Carnevale, Gulish, and Campbell, *If Not Now, When*, 6.
6. Carl Benedict Frey and Michael A. Osborne, "The Future of Employment: How Susceptible Are Jobs to Computerisation?" (working paper, Oxford Martin School, University of Oxford, Oxford, England, 2013).
7. Elizabeth Mann Levesque, *Understanding the Skills Gap—and What Employers Can Do About It*, Employer Perspectives on Workforce Development (Washington, DC: Brookings Institution, 2019). https://www.brookings.edu/research/understanding-the-skills-gap-and-what-employers-can-do-about-it/.

8. Robert D. Putnam, *The Upswing: How America Came Together a Century Ago and How We Can Do It Again*. (New York: Simon & Schuster, 2020), chapter 2.
9. California Department of Education, California School Dashboard. https://www.caschooldashboard.org/reports/30664310000000/2020. All data are from 2020, the most recent available at the time of this writing.
10. Adapted from Michael B. Matsuda, "I'm a Superintendent: My Students' Activism is Key to Their Academic Success," *Education Week*, March 3, 2020.
11. Information about GEAR UP is located at https://www2.ed.gov/programs/gearup/index.html.
12. We present this origin story for the district's major reform ideas and values in more detail in chapter 2.
13. This chapter presents vision, mission, and core values as general concepts. In chapter 2 we explain in detail how the vision was developed as part of systems thinking. See https://auhsd.us/ for the vision statement.
14. More detail about the process of developing the vision is provided in chapter 2.
15. https://www.auhsd.us/District/Department/14175-SUPERINTENDENT-S-OFFICE/88182-Mission.html chapter 2.
16. See chrome-extension://efaidnbmnnnibpcajpcglclefindmkaj/https://www.auhsd.us/files/user/1/file/AUHSD%20Mission%2C%20Vision%2C%20Core%203.pdf/. Emphasis in the original.
17. Peter M. Senge, *The Fifth Discipline: The Art and Practice of the Learning Organization* (New York: Doubleday, 2006); Fred Kofman, *Conscious Business: How to Build Value Through Values* (Boulder, CO: Sounds True, 2013).
18. Senge, *The Fifth Discipline*, 132, 139–144.
19. We elaborate on systems thinking and what that means in AUHSD in chapter 2.
20. We elaborate our theories of action in chapters 2 and 3.
21. See https://auhsd.us/District/Department/14207-ANAHEIM-UHSD/85623-Career-Preparedness-Systems-Framework-CPSF.html.
22. Each of the aspects of the CPSF addressed here in general terms is detailed in subsequent chapters.
23. See https://auhsd.us/District/Department/14207-ANAHEIM-UHSD/85623-Career-Preparedness-Systems-Framework-CPSF.html. Terms familiar in AUHSD may introduce an element of ambiguity for some readers. Twenty-first-century skills have to do with how students and adults relate to one another and work together. They are rooted in psychological and emotional stability and lead to a higher degree of social success, particularly in the workplace. Commonly in education, this kind of development within students is labeled as affective, or addressing emotions and feelings, to draw a distinction from cognitive development, which we equate with technical skills.
24. The 5Cs and their accompanying rubrics can be found by scrolling down on this webpage: https://auhsd.us/District/Department/14207-ANAHEIM-UHSD/85623-Career-Preparedness-Systems-Framework-CPSF.html.
25. "Elevated voice and purpose" is a phrase that captures AUHSD's complex goal that students will be able to manage their lives in a fulfilling manner by the time they leave high school. Brief discussion of similar ideas can be found here: https://michaelfullan.ca/our-increasingly-troubled-world-creates-an-engaging-opportunity-for-students/.
26. Both are elaborated in chapter 2.
27. "Workforce Indicators Report," Orange County Business Council, https://ocbc.org/research/workforce-indicators-report/.

CHAPTER 2

1. The quotation, attributed to Ackoff, is ubiquitous on the internet and can be found here: https://www.azquotes.com/quote/1077419.
2. This phrase is a Buddhist saying that is attributed to an anonymous author. It is close in meaning to a quotation attributed to Roman emperor Marcus Aurelius: "The impediment to action advances action. What stands in the way becomes the way." Some confusion may be caused by the title of a popular book that contains the phrase, "The obstacle is the way." Our use of the phrase exemplifies the AUHSD approach to obstacles potentially impeding the CPSF.
3. Peter N. Senge, *The Fifth Discipline: The Art and Practice of the Learning Organization*, revised ed. (New York: Currency, 2006); Russell L. Ackoff, *Ackoff's Best: His Classic Writings on Management* (New York: John Wiley and Sons, Inc., 1999), chapter 2. Note that our use of the term "systems thinking" derives from Senge. We extend Senge's definition using some of his original sources and the organizational leadership literature.
4. Families are another "system of interest," but introducing them here complicates the framework in ways difficult to handle in the narrative of this chapter. We defer discussing families and their role in the CPSF until chapter 6, when we explain the district's implementation of Community Schools.
5. Michael Fullan, *The Principal: Three Keys to Maximizing Impact* (San Francisco: Jossey-Bass, 2014).
6. Ackoff, *Ackoff's Best*, 40–41.
7. Ackoff, *Ackoff's Best*, 40–41.
8. To avoid awkward differentiations, we speak often of the principal's role while implying that "principal" extends to the administrative team because of principals' delegation of work.
9. Fred Kofman, *Conscious Business: How to Build Value Through Values* (Boulder, CO: SoundsTrue, 2013), chapter 4.
10. Robert G. Smith and S. David Brazer, *Striving for Equity: District Leadership for Narrowing Opportunity and Achievement Gaps* (Cambridge, MA: Harvard Education Press, 2016), chapters 3–5.
11. "Herb Peterson," Wikipedia, last modified October 22, 2022, https://en.wikipedia.org/wiki/Herb_Peterson.
12. Justin Worland, "McDonald's to Switch to Cage-Free Eggs," *Time*, September 9, 2015, https://time.com/4026501/mcdonalds-cage-free/.
13. We provide test score evidence of student outcomes in chapter 4.
14. One of the original explanations of organizations as open systems comes from James D. Thompson, *Organizations in Action: Social Science Bases of Administrative Theory* (New Brunswick, NJ: Transaction Publishers, 2008). For very accessible discussion of open systems and how these concepts fit into the larger field of organization theory, see W. Richard Scott, *Organizations: Rational, Natural, and Open Systems*, 5th ed. (Upper Saddle River, NJ: Prentice Hall, 2003).
15. Muench was the chief marketing officer at Yum! Brands, which served numerous large corporate clients including KFC, Pizza Hut, and Taco Bell. For more on its marketing approaches, see Greg Creed and Ken Muench, *R.E.D. Marketing: The Three Ingredients of Leading Brands* (New York: HarperCollins Leadership, 2021).
16. March and Simon said it best: "Effective control over organizational process is limited . . . by the uncertainties and ambiguities of life, by the limited cognitive and affective capabilities of human actors, by the complexities of balancing trade-offs across time

and space, and by threats of competition." James G. March and Herbert A. Simon, *Organizations* (Cambridge, MA: Blackwell, 1993), 2. Larry Cuban provides a persuasive argument for why schools are complex in *Inside the Black Box of Classroom Practice: Change Without Reform in American Education* (Cambridge, MA: Harvard Education Press, 2013).
17. Senge, *The Fifth Discipline*, 63–64.
18. Senge, *The Fifth Discipline*, 64.
19. "Trim tabs are small surfaces connected to the trailing edge of a larger control surface on a boat or aircraft, used to control the trim of the controls, i.e., to counteract hydro- or aerodynamic forces and stabilize the boat or aircraft in a particular desired attitude without the need for the operator to constantly apply a control force. This is done by adjusting the angle of the tab relative to the larger surface." From "Trim Tab," Wikipedia, last modified December 13, 2022, https://en.wikipedia.org/wiki/Trim_tab.
20. Michael Fullan and Joanne Quinn, *Coherence: The Right Drivers in Action for Schools, Districts, and Systems* (Thousand Oaks, CA: Corwin, 2015), chapter 1.
21. This bridging activity is discussed in terms of specific programs and partnerships in chapters 4 and 6.
22. Thompson, *Organizations in Action*.
23. Senge, *The Fifth Discipline*, 132.
24. Kofman, *Conscious Business*, 10.
25. See chapter 6.
26. Senge, *The Fifth Discipline*, 129.
27. Chris Argyris and Donald A. Schön, *Theory in Practice: Increasing Professional Effectiveness* (San Francisco: Jossey-Bass, 1974).
28. Kofman, *Conscious Business*, 12.
29. Ackoff, *Ackoff's Best*, 36–41.
30. Kurt Lewin, "Frontiers in Group Dynamics: Concept, Reality, and Method in Social Science; Social Equilibria and Social Change," *Human Relations* 1, no. 5 (1947): 5–41, doi: 10.1177/001872674700100103.
31. Marvin R. Weisbord, *Productive Workplaces Revisited: Dignity, Meaning, and Community in the 21st Century* (San Francisco: Jossey-Bass, 2004), 255.
32. Weisbord, *Productive Workplaces Revisited*, 255–56.
33. Chris Argyris and Donald A. Schön, *Organizational Learning II: Theory, Method, and Practice* (Reading, MA: Addison-Wesley, 1996), 20–25.
34. Single-loop learning has value for education organizations, but the CPSF is a substantial change in the status quo, which is why we focus our attention on double-loop learning.
35. See Scott C. Bauer and S. David Brazer, *Using Research to Lead School Improvement: Turning Evidence into Action* (Thousand Oaks, CA: SAGE Publications, 2012), chapter 6, for a more detailed application of root cause analysis to school improvement.
36. Regina Powers to David Brazer, personal communication, June 2, 2022.
37. We discuss the role of dual enrollment in the CPSF in chapter 4.
38. More detail about signature programs within the CPSF is provided in chapter 4.
39. "The California Democracy School Project . . . is designed to institutionalize civic learning in elementary, middle, or high schools to prepare ALL students for college, career, and citizenship in the 21st century." In "California Democracy School Civic Learning

Initiative," Los Angeles County Office of Education, https://www.lacoe.edu/Curriculum-Instruction/History-Social-Science/California-Democracy-School.
40. S. David Brazer, Scott C. Bauer, and Bob L. Johnson Jr., *Leading Schools to Learn, Grow, and Thrive: Using Theory to Strengthen Practice* (New York: Routledge, 2019); Phillip Hallinger, "Leading Educational Change: Reflections on the Practice of Instructional and Transformational Leadership," *Cambridge Journal of Education* 33, no. 3 (2003): 329–51; Viviane M. J. Robinson, Claire A. Lloyd, and Kenneth J. Rowe, "The Impact of Leadership on Student Outcomes: An Analysis of the Differential Effects of Leadership Types," *Educational Administration Quarterly* 44, no. 5 (2008): 635–74; Kenneth Leithwood, Alma Harris, and David Hopkins, "Seven Strong Claims About Successful School Leadership," *School Leadership and Management* 28, no. 1 (2008): 27–42.
41. School site cabinets are the site-level version of the superintendent's cabinet.
42. Robinson, Lloyd, and Rowe explain that this behavior has the highest effect size among the varied leader behaviors they identified in their meta-analysis.
43. Chris Argyris and Donald A. Schön, *Organizational Learning II: Theory, Method, and Practice* (Reading, MA: Addison-Wesley, 1978), chapter 1.

CHAPTER 3

1. Larry Cuban, *The Managerial Imperative and the Practice of Leadership in Schools* (Albany: State University of New York Press, 1988).
2. Continuation high schools are regulated by the California Education Code. Their most common students are truant from their comprehensive high schools to the extent they have insufficient credit to be promoted to the next grade level. Students who have chronic misbehavior or are under an expulsion order suspended by the school board may also attend a continuation high school. The expectation is that students will make up lost credit within a semester or year and return to the school from which they were transferred. About 50 percent of AUHSD's continuation high school students return to their home schools. Most of the remaining half graduates from the continuation high school.
3. The percentages do not account for all demographic descriptors and will not add to 100% because of students being counted in more than one category. The graph is intended to show relative proportions to provide a sense of the magnitude of various student groups.
4. Robert. G. Smith and S. David Brazer, *Striving for Equity: District Leadership for Narrowing Opportunity and Achievement Gaps* (Cambridge, MA: Harvard Education Press, 2016).
5. "Data Quest," California Department of Education, https://dq.cde.ca.gov/dataquest/.
6. Abraham H. Maslow, "A Theory of Human Motivation," *Psychological Review* 50, no. 4 (1943): 370–96.
7. See, for example, Frederick Herzberg, Bernard Mausner, and Barbara Bloch Snyderman, *The Motivation to Work* (New Brunswick, NJ: Transaction Publishers, 1959 and 1993), 107–19.
8. Carl Frey and Michael Osborne, "The Future of Employment: How Susceptible Are Jobs to Computerisation?" *Technological Forecasting* 114 (2013): 254–80.
9. Elizabeth Mann Levesque, "Employer Perspectives on Workforce Development: How Businesses are Adapting to the Future of Work," Brookings Institute, December 6, 2019,

https://www.brookings.edu/multi-chapter-report/employer-perspectives-on-workforce-development-how-businesses-are-adapting-to-the-future-of-work/.

CHAPTER 4

1. "Percentage of employed women in computing-related occupations in the United States from 2007 to 2020, by ethnicity," Statista, https://www.statista.com/statistics/311967/us-women-computer-workers-ethnicity/#:~:text=In%202020%2C%20women%20of%20color,persons%20employed%20in%20these%20occupations.
2. Rachel Carson, *Silent Spring* (Boston: Harper Collins, 2022), 140.
3. Michael Fullan and Joanne Quinn, *Coherence: The Right Drivers for in Action for Schools, Districts, and Systems* (Thousand Oaks, CA: Corwin, 2015).
4. Fullan and Quinn, *Coherence*.
5. Test administration was in the spring of the year named. The tests were not administered in California during the pandemic year of 2020–2021.
6. "Smarter Balanced Test Results: State of California," EdSource, http://caaspp.edsource.org/sbac/statewide?_gl=1*et3q65*_ga*MTg3NTMxODUyNi4xNjY1Njg4NTcy*_ga_475QR6J62K*MTY2ODgwNTQ5Ni41LjAuMTY2ODgwNTQ5Ni42MC4wLjA.
7. See, for example, this issue of "The Nation's Report Card" that discusses recent NAEP scores. In 2022, fourth graders had the highest proficiency rates in math, followed by eighth graders, followed by high school seniors. See https://www.nationsreportcard.gov/mathematics/nation/achievement/?grade=4.
8. Joe Hong and Erica Yee, "California student test scores plunge—but some achievement gaps narrow. See how your school compares," *CalMatters*, October 24, 2022, https://calmatters.org/education/k-12-education/2022/10/california-student-test-scores-dive-district-lookup/.
9. Hanneh Bareham and Chelsea Wing, "2022 College Graduation Statistics," Bankrate, May 9, 2022, https://www.bankrate.com/loans/student-loans/college-graduation-statistics/. See for discussion of college graduation statistics from 2022.
10. Cypress High School had 42.79% low-income students in 2021–2022, and Kennedy had 56.85%. Anaheim High School had 90.74% low-income students.
11. Julianna Hernandez and Mariana Gomez, "CSU Fullerton: Partner Update for Anaheim Collaborative," March 29, 2022, https://drive.google.com/file/d/1DkYqA-QTx20BVz71I3Hik3V6WqQvNl74/view.
12. Santana Ruiz to Michael Matsuda, personal communication, September 5, 2022.
13. "AUHSD Educational Pledge," https://www.auhsd.us/District/Department/14186-Curriculum-Instruction/Portal/auhsd-educational-pledge for Pledge details.
14. Ashley A. Smith, Daniel J. Willis, and Yuxuan Xie, "Growing numbers of California high schoolers dual enroll in college courses, but access uneven statewide," *EdSource*, November 10, 2022, https://edsource.org/2022/growing-numbers-of-california-high-schoolers-dual-enroll-in-college-courses-but-access-uneven-statewide/680331.
15. Robert P. Moses and Charles E. Cobb, *Radical Equations* (Boston: Beacon Press, 2002), 5.
16. Larry Cuban, *Confessions of a School Reformer* (Cambridge, MA: Harvard Education Press, 2021), 13–15.
17. CTE and internships fall under the general category of "work-based learning." Internships are part of career training that involves various levels of engagement. For simplicity of explanation, we use the term "internship" to cover any student experience that is school supported and involves regular attendance and work in a setting outside of

school. Internships are distinct from general work experience programs in that they are based in the CTE curriculum and promoted by AIME coordinators.
18. Note that we report percentages of the student subgroup. We indicate in figure 4.9, for example, that 80% of homeless students at Anaheim High School participate in CTE; we mean 80% of the homeless population at AHS, which in 2021–2022 was 197 students.
19. Note that we have omitted Gilbert High School (the district's continuation high school) and Oxford Academy (an academic magnet school) because as special programs, these schools are not representative of the typical student experience in the district.
20. Henry Hua, personal communication to Michael Matsuda, March 27, 2022.
21. Tim Nguyen, personal communication to Michael Matsuda, March 27, 2022.
22. It is worth nothing that cybersecurity is only one of six pathways available at Magnolia High School. There is ample opportunity for career exploration in a variety of fields.
23. Jamie Kaledjian to Michael Matsuda, personal communication during visit from the Surry School District to AUHSD, October 27, 2022.
24. See chapter 2 and below.
25. Gareth Cook, "The Economist Who Would Fix the American Dream." *Atlantic,* July 17, 2019, https://www.theatlantic.com/magazine/archive/2019/08/raj-chettys-american-dream/592804/.
26. Alana Semuels, "America's Lost Einsteins," *Atlantic,* December 4, 2017, https://www.theatlantic.com/business/archive/2017/12/innovation-income-chetty/547202/.
27. Semuels, "America's Lost Einsteins."
28. AIME is explained in the next section.
29. See brief descriptions and Mayor Tom Tait's responses in chapters 1 and 2.
30. Information about eKadence is available at https://www.ekadence.org/.
31. Mike Switzer to David Brazer, personal communication, May 24, 2022.

CHAPTER 5

1. John Dewey, *Democracy and Education: An Introduction to the Philosophy of Education* (New York: Free Press, 1916/1944), 351.
2. Abraham H. Maslow, "A Theory of Human Motivation," *Psychological Review* 50, no. 4 (1943): 370–96.
3. Progressive educators who agreed with Dewey in the late nineteenth and early twentieth centuries saw themselves as part of a larger social and political movement to address the needs of immigrants and the poor. Not to be confused with the Administrative Progressives from the same era who were focused on accountability and testing, Dewey and the instruction-focused Progressives pursued experiential learning and the integration of schools into society as a means to uplift the immigrant poor. They are in many ways the intellectual forebears of the CPSF. The term "Progressive" has taken on a different meaning in twenty-first-century politics. See Larry Cuban, David Tyack, and other education historians for more detailed descriptions of Progressives of all types in education during the period of fast industrialization and large waves of immigration.
4. See chapter 1 for a discussion of the 4Cs promoted by P21.
5. "Dopamine," Health Direct, https://www.healthdirect.gov.au/dopamine#:~:text=of%20the%20brain.-,What%20is%20the%20role%20of%20dopamine%3F,of%20dopamine%20in%20the%20brain.
6. Christine M. Sabler, "The Effects of Social Media on Mental Health," LG Health Hub, Penn Medicine, Lancaster General Health, September 1, 2021, https://www.lancaster

generalhealth.org/health-hub-home/2021/september/the-effects-of-social-media-on-mental-health.
7. See Viktor E. Frankl, *Man's Search for Meaning*, rev. ed. (New York: Washington Square Press, 1984); Maslow, "A Theory of Human Motivation."
8. Dr. Home Nguyen, personal communication to Michael Matsuda, October 21, 2022.
9. Sarah Suatoni, personal communication to Michael Matsuda, October 9, 2022.
10. Dr. Home Nguyen, personal communication, October 21, 2022.
11. Sharon D. Kruse, *Mindful Educational Leadership: Contemplative, Cognitive, and Organizational Systems and Practices* (New York: Routledge, 2023).
12. Fred Kofman, *Conscious Business: How to Build Value Through Values* (Boulder, CO: Sounds True, 2002) provides insight into concepts such as emotional intelligence and conscious communication. For original work on emotional intelligence, see Daniel Goleman, *Emotional Intelligence: Why it Can Matter More than IQ* (New York: Bantam Books, 2006).
13. Katrina Mundy, used with permission.

CHAPTER 6

1. Brené Brown, "Why Your Critics Aren't the Ones Who Count" (speech, 99U Conferences), https://www.youtube.com/watch?v=8-JXOnFOXQk.
2. Morgan Smith, "'It Killed My Spirit': How 3 Teachers Are Navigating the Burnout Crisis in Education," CNBC MakeIt, November 22, 2022, https://www.cnbc.com/2022/11/22/teachers-are-in-the-midst-of-a-burnout-crisis-it-became-intolerable.html. See for an estimate of 300,000 teachers and other staff leaving education in 2022.
3. Richard F. Elmore, *School Reform from the Inside Out: Policy, Practice, and Performance* (Cambridge, MA: Harvard Education Press, 2004), 92–93.
4. Diana Fujimoto to David Brazer, personal communication, December 9, 2022. This section is based on communications between Fujimoto and Brazer.
5. See Elizabeth A. City et al., *Instructional Rounds in Education: A Network Approach to Improving Teaching and Learning* (Cambridge, MA: Harvard Education Press, 2009), chapter 1. By "instructional core," City et al. mean the interactions among the teacher, the student, and the curriculum. See also Lee S. Shulman, *The Wisdom of Practice: Essays on Teaching, Learning, and Learning to Teach* (San Francisco: Jossey-Bass, 2004), chapter 6. Our understanding of pedagogical content knowledge comes primarily from the chapter referenced and personal communication with Shulman, who coined the term. More complex than City et al.'s explanation of the instructional core, Shulman's ideas are informed by the work of Joseph Schwab, who argued that to understand the classroom requires knowing about the simultaneous influences and interactions of the student, the teacher, the content, and the context. Shulman refines this fundamental idea to explain that, in proficient teaching, content and pedagogy interact in ways that address the needs of a specific student audience.
6. A. Maier, J. Daniel, and J. Oakes, "Community Schools as an Effective School Improvement Strategy: A Review of the Evidence," research brief (Palo Alto, CA: Learning Policy Institute, 2017).
7. This quotation is taken from the state teacher association newsletter. Emphasis added. "Member Spotlight," *CTA and You*, December 15, 2022.
8. "Member Spotlight," *CTA and You*.
9. This and the following quotations are from a video AUHSD made to capture teachers' externship experiences. See https://www.youtube.com/watch?v=mBBkbCJ6864.

10. See chapters 1 and 2.
11. Kelly Gallagher to David Brazer, personal communication, December 12, 2022. For an explanation of the reasons for the Writing Journey and how it worked, see Kelly Gallagher, "The Writing Journey," *Educational Leadership* 7, no. 5 (2017): 24–29.
12. See https://tdtrust.org/what-is-lesson-study/ for a brief explanation of Lesson Study and links to additional resources.
13. The concept of the Four-Room Apartment originates with Janssen, according to Weisbord. See Marvin R. Weisbord, *Productive Workplaces Revisited*, 2nd ed. (New York: John Wiley & Sons), 333–35. Our discussion departs from Weisbord's because we perceive the challenges to making change somewhat differently.
14. Michael Fullan, *Leading in a Culture of Change*, 2nd ed. (San Francisco: Jossey-Bass, 2020).

CHAPTER 7

1. Paolo Freire, *Pedagogy of the Oppressed*, 50th anniversary ed. (New York: Bloomsbury Academic).
2. Schlechty was a nationally renowned education reformer from the 1980s to the 2000s. He was a key architect of statewide reforms in Tennessee and North Carolina. The quotation is as Brazer remembers it from a presentation Schlechty made at the Santa Clara County (CA) Office of Education, 1995.
3. Frank Cottle, "Lisa Gevelber Founder of Grow with Google: Transforming the Economy Through Education," podcast, July 28, 2022, https://allwork.space/2022/07/lisa-gevelber-founder-of-grow-with-google-transforming-the-economy-through-education/.
4. We acknowledge T. J. Vari, assistant superintendent in the Appoquinimink (DE) School District, for this vivid image.
5. For more detail about VUCA, see Nate Bennett and G. James Lemoine, "What VUCA Really Means for You," *Harvard Business Review*, January-February 2022.
6. Cal Newport, "The Year in Quiet Quitting: A New Generation Discovers It's Hard to Balance Work with a Well-Lived Life," *New Yorker*, December 29, 2022, https://www.newyorker.com/culture/2022-in-review/the-year-in-quiet-quitting.
7. Jim Harter, "Is Quiet Quitting Real?" Gallup, September 6, 2022, https://www.gallup.com/workplace/398306/quiet-quitting-real.aspx.
8. Douglas McGregor, *The Human Side of Enterprise*, annotated ed. (New York: McGraw-Hill, 2006), 48–64; 346–49.
9. John Dewey, *Experience and Education* (New York: Touchstone, 1938/1997), 62.
10. This quotation can be found on many internet websites, including: https://www.azquotes.com/quote/349611.

APPENDIX B

1. See https://teach.mikvachallenge.org/unit/creating-democratic-classrooms for more information.

ACKNOWLEDGMENTS

The process of writing this book has been a profound learning experience for the two of us. Our friendship has blossomed through this collaboration. And we didn't do it alone.

We wish to thank the Harvard Education Press staff for their support throughout the writing and publication process. It all began with Jayne Fargnoli's enthusiasm and encouragement for the initially vague idea for a book about major reform in an urban school district. Her reassurance as editor in chief energized our passion for telling this story. Shannon Davis, our acquisitions editor, has been a steadfast friend and compassionate critic. When we felt tentative or uncertain, she helped put us to get back on course with insightful comments and warm inspiration that sprang from her reviews of chapters in draft.

Many AUHSD educators were generous with their time as we asked them for help to tell the truth about what has succeeded and what remains a work in progress. Erik Greenwood and Charles Ku gave us essential data and guided us in our quest for more. Manuel Colon, Mary Jo (MJ) Cooke, Jackie Counts, Diana Fujimoto, Kelly Gallagher, Regina Powers, Scott Reindl, and Mike Switzer participated in lengthy interviews that provided multiple perspectives essential to generating a shared reality that comes as close to truth as we can get. Amanda Bean and Amy Kwon gave us even more data and provided important insights from both the school and district points of view. All AUHSD personnel were patient and tireless whenever we asked them questions about what really goes on inside the district and the schools.

Anyone who has ever attempted long-form writing such as this knows that it is possible to get lost in your own head; coauthors can create shared insulation from critique. We are grateful to friends and colleagues who took time from their busy lives to review emerging ideas and drafts of chapters. Brian Ahn, Scott Bauer, John Bautista, Brian Brady, Jaron Fried, Scott Reindl, and Bill Rich served us as true critical friends.

Despite all of this wonderful help, we know we have made some mistakes and we own them as we strive to be better and do better every day.

ABOUT THE AUTHORS

S. David Brazer (PhD, Stanford University) is a former secondary school teacher, high school principal, and university professor. He is the author of numerous peer-reviewed articles and three books: *Leading Schools to Learn, Grow, and Thrive* (Routledge, 2019), *Striving for Equity* (Harvard Education Press, 2016), and *Using Research to Lead School Improvement* (SAGE, 2012). Theoretical publications relevant to this book include: "Leaders as Bricoleurs: Sensemaking as a Pathway to Skillful Leadership" (2019), "Structural Perspectives on Schools as Organizations" (with Scott Bauer, 2018), and "Analyzing Learning in Professional Learning Communities: A Conceptual Framework" (with Michelle Van Lare, 2013). Recent empirical publications focused on exploration of the work of teacher collaborative teams inform Brazer's understanding of district initiatives focused on improving the student experience. He is principal consultant at Brazer Education Consulting, LLC.

Michael B. Matsuda is the superintendent of the Anaheim Union High School District (2014–present). Starting his education career as a long-term substitute, Matsuda has served as a junior high school and high school English teacher. Central office work prior to becoming superintendent included preparing and supporting new teachers and administering large federal grants. He has also served on the local community college board of trustees. All of his work in education has focused on fostering equity for low-income students of color and students from immigrant families. Matsuda is the recipient of numerous awards and recognitions including one of thirteen "Leaders to Learn From" from *Education Week*; a "Visionary Leader" award from Cal State University, Fullerton School of Education; the California State "Champion of Civics" award; and the University of California, Irvine School of Education "Outstanding Community Partner" award. Additionally, he received an honorary doctorate from Chapman University in 2015 for his work in education.

INDEX

Abby (student), 61–62, 63
abiguity, 40
Ackoff, Russell L., 27, 29–30, 32
administrative teams, 55–56, 159
affective development. *See* twenty-first-century skills
AIME (Anaheim Innovative Mentoring Experience), 100–106, 167
AIME Teacher Externships, 138–139
Alaysia (student), 79, 98–99
ambiguity, 152–153
Anaheim Educational Collaborative, 87–90, 150, 167
Anaheim Educational Pledge, 87–90
Anaheim Union High School District (AUHSD). *See also* Capstone projects; career and technical education (CTE); career pathways; Career Preparedness Systems Framework (CPSF); dual-enrollment programs; partnerships; student voice and purpose; systems thinking
  overview of, 13
  demographics of, 62–70
  superintendent at, 13–15
  vision, mission, and core values of, 15–18, 20–21
Anjelica (student), 10–11, 76
Anthony (student), 10–11, 76
Argyris, Chris, 50
arrogance, 33–34
autonomy/coherence balance, 34–35, 67–68
Axel (student), 63–64

belonging, 72–73
branded houses, 38–40

branding, 38–40
bricklayers parable, 155
bridging to resources, 36–37, 44, 50–52
Brown, Brené, 129
buffering against threats, 36–37, 44
businesses, partnerships with, 22–23
buy-in, 89–90

cabinets, 55–56, 159
Calleros, Ruben, 63–64
calling, finding, 155–156
Capstone projects
  overview of, 20–21
  level-two illustrated by, 108–109
  playbook for, 164
  professional learning and, 133–134
  student voice and purpose elevated by, 111–114
  systems thinking and, 53–54
  theory of change embedded in, 113
career and technical education (CTE). *See also* career pathways
  gender and, 97–98
  history of, 90–91
  participation rates, 94
  pathways available at district, 91–95
  reverse engineering of pathways for, 95–100
  use of at AUHSD, 21–22
  vocational education compared, 91
career pathways
  choices available at district, 95–100
  cybersecurity pathway, 95–100, 138
  dual-enrollment programs and, 22
  funding for, 138
  future envisioned with, 21–22, 73–75

career pathways (*continued*)
   Google Career Certificates, 148–150
   internships for, 79
   mentorship and, 101
   professional learning and, 136–138
   reverse engineering of CTE pathways, 95–100
Career Preparedness Systems Framework (CPSF). *See also* career pathways; partnerships; student voice and purpose; technical skills; twenty-first century skills
   adapting to student needs, 67–68
   challenges for, 148
   elements of, 18–24, 76
   leadership needed for, 157–158
   logic of, 75–76
   need for, 147–151
   patience needed for, 160–161
   reflection on, 161
   strategic positioning for, 151–156
   theory of action for, 56–57
   white paper on, 163
Carl Perkins money, 138
Carson, Rachel, 80
central office. *See* school districts and district offices
certificates, 148–150
change
   as messy, 157
   patience needed for, 160–161
   reflection on, 116, 161
   resistance and motivation, 47–49, 141–145, 158
   trim tabs and, 41–44
   unfreezing concept, 48–49
Chetty, Raj, 2, 98, 99
choices, 117, 120, 155
Cindy, 72
civic engagement, 23, 28, 53
classrooms, social systems lens in, 72–73
coaches, 41–42, 54, 107–109, 133–134
cognitive development, 21–23, 29
cognitive mindfulness, 122
coherence/autonomy balance, 34–35, 67–68
Coherence (Fullan and Quinn), 80–81
Collar, Jason, 139
college admission and enrollment, 84–87

community, 35–38, 42–43
community college, 22, 51, 107
Community Schools, 134–137, 153
Complacency Room, 142–143
complexity, 153
compliance, 154
Confusion Room, 143–144, 157
contemplative mindfulness, 122
control, 33–34
Cooke, Mary Jo (MJ), 105
core values of AUHSD, 15–18, 20–21
COVID-19 pandemic impacts, 27, 152–153
CPSF. *See* Career Preparedness Systems Framework (CPSF)
creative tension, 17, 45–47, 50
CTE. *See* career and technical education (CTE)
CTE pathways. *See* career pathways
Cuban, Larry, 7
curriculum specialists
   professional learning and, 131, 132–134
   systems thinking and, 33, 107
   as trim tab leaders, 42, 54
cybersecurity pathway, 95–100, 138

data management, 109
decisional capital, 31, 32
Democracy Schools program, 53, 167
demographics, 62–70, 78
Denial Room, 143
department chairs, 56, 108
Dewey, John, 117, 154
disabilities, students with
   AIME participation, 102–105
   in AUHSD, 69–70
   Axel, 63–64
   CTE pathways participation, 91–94
   cybersecurity pathway participation, 96–97
   dual-enrollment participation, 88–89
   iLab participation, 101
discrimination, Japanese internment camps and, 1–2
dissatisfaction with work, 152–156
district office. *See* school districts and district offices
district of schools versus school district, 34, 39

dopamine, 119
double-loop learning, 50–51, 57
dual-enrollment programs
    career pathways and, 22
    college preparation from, 83–84
    expansion of, 88–90
    student voice and purpose and, 107
    textbook adoption process changes needed for, 51
economic inequality, structural inequality and, 2
economic mobility, marginalized groups and, 2
educational experiences, differences over time, 9–11
educational pathways, importance of, 11. *See also* career pathways
eKadence, 109, 164
Elder, Dean, 89–90
Elmore, Richard, 130–131
empathy, 124–125
employability gap, 9, 74
English language arts (ELA) test scores, 81–82
English language learners
    AIME participation, 102–105
    in AUHSD, 65–66
    CTE pathways participation, 93–94
    cybersecurity pathway participation, 96–97
    dual-enrollment participation, 88–89
    iLab participation, 101
enrollment declines, funding and, 44
environmental issues, 80
equity
    AIME participation, 102–105
    CTE pathways and, 91–94
    dual-enrollment programs and, 89
    iLab and, 99, 101
ethnic categories, proportions of, 68–69
Executive Order 9066, 1, 13
externships for teachers, 138–139

family assets, 150–151
feedback loops, 47–48
The Fifth Discipline (Senge), 29
5Cs
    compassion added to, 118
    CPSF and, 19–20
    defined, 16
    hygiene factors and, 73
    mindfulness to achieve, 125–126
    rubric for, 164
    six Cs compared, 81
    trim tabs and, 41–42
    vision, mission, and core values and, 20–21
5Cs coaches, 41–42, 54, 107–109, 133–134
flaws as unnoticed, 150
for-profit enterprises, CTE pathways and, 107
foster youth, 69
Four-Room Apartment model of change, 141–145, 152–153, 157
franchise construct, 34
Frankl, Viktor, 120–121
Freire, Paolo, 147
Fried, Jaron, 89–90
Fujimoto, Diana, 132
Fullan, Michael, 31, 80–81, 165
funding, 44, 138, 148, 167–168

Gallagher, Kelly, 139–141
GEAR UP, 167–168
gender, cybersecurity pathway participation, 97–98
Gevelber, Lisa, 148–149
Google Career Certificates, 148–150
governing variables, 57
grassroots professional learning, 139–141

Herzberg, Frederick, 71
hierarchy of needs, 70–71
higher education, 8–11, 22
Home, Dr., 118–123
homeless students
    AIME participation, 102–105
    in AUHSD, 65, 67
    CTE pathways participation, 93–94
    cybersecurity pathway participation, 96–97
    dual-enrollment participation, 88–89
    iLab participation, 101
    schools needing to adapt to needs of, 61–62
Hua, Henry, 95

humility, 33–34, 122
hygiene factors, 71–72, 73

iLab, 98–101, 168
Illumination Institute, 123
income level within district, 62–63. *See also* low-income students
Inflexion, 163
influence loops, 47–48
influencers, 56, 108, 135–136. *See also* 5Cs coaches
innovative neighborhoods, 98–99
instructional leadership, 52–56, 99–100, 110
internships and mentorship, 22–23, 72, 79, 97–99, 100–106
It, We, and I schema, 17–18, 45–47

Japanese internment camps, 1, 13
jobs, elimination of by technology, 9, 74

Keledjian, Jamie, 97–98
Khan, Zaid, 153–154
Kim, Jeff, 139
King, Martin Luther, Jr., 155
Kofman, Fred, 17, 33–34, 45–47
Kruse, Sharon, 122

learning management systems, 109
learning organizations, 45–52
Learning Policy Institute, 135
Lesson Study, 140
leverage principle, 41
Lewin, Kurt, 48, 144
life readiness, what constitutes, 81
Logotherapy, 120–121
low-income students
    AIME participation, 102–105
    in AUHSD, 62–63, 65–66
    college admission and enrollment, 84–85
    CTE pathways participation, 93–94
    dual-enrollment participation, 88–89
    English language arts (ELA) test scores, 82
    increase in number of, 9

MACC, 168
Magnolia Cybersecurity Institute, 96–97
Man's Search for Meaning (Frankl), 120–121

Manzanar internment camp, 1
marginalized groups. *See* disabilities, students with; English language learners; homeless students; low-income students
Maslow's hierarchy of needs, 70–71
math test scores, 81, 83
Matsuda, Michael B., 13–15, 61, 118–121
McDonald's, 34
meaningful work. *See* career pathways; workforce development
mental health, 120, 123
mentorship and internships, 22–23, 72, 79, 97–99, 100–106
MeridianLink, 95–96
mindfulness, 117–127
MindKind Institute, 121–123
mission of AUHSD, 15–18, 20–21
Moses, Bob, 7, 90
motivation, 70–73, 153–156
Muench, Ken, 38–40
Muñoz, Rafael, 155–156

Naranjo, Christie, 139
narrative
    overview of, 7–8
    empowering graduates, 18–24
    importance of, 158–159
    purpose and, 11–13
    reflection on, 35
    taking stock of, 25
    vision, mission, and core values and, 15–18
network building. *See* partnerships
Nguyen, Home H. C., 118–123
Nguyen, Tim, 95–96, 109, 138–139
nonprofits, 22–23, 107

ontological arrogance, 33–34
ontological humility, 33–34, 122
open systems, 43–44, 50–52
organizational learning, 45–52, 99–100, 122

P21 Partnership, 19
parents as assets, 150–151
partnerships
    AIME, 104–106

Anaheim Educational Collaborative, 87–90
   CTE pathway creation and, 94–100
   funding and, 148
   with higher education, 22
   with nonprofit and business partners, 22–23
   politics and, 159–160
   reflection on, 116
   trim tabs and, 43
patience, 160–161
Patino, Reuben, 53
performance task assessments (PTAs), 108–109. *See also* Capstone projects
personal mastery, 47, 122
Peterson, Herb, 34
politics, importance of, 159–160
portfolios. *See* Capstone projects
poverty. *See* low-income students
The Principal (Fullan), 31–32
principals, 33, 55–56, 157–158, 160
professional learning
   overview of, 129–130, 145
   avenues for, 130–141
   reflection on, 146
professional learning teams, 55–56
purpose, 11–13, 29, 152–156. *See also* student voice and purpose

quiet quitting, 153–156
Quinn, Joanne, 80–81

reality, 45
reform, challenges for, 151–152
Reindl, Scott, 104–105, 138
Renewal Room, 144
residence requirements, 62
Rodriguez, Jemma, 136
Roosevelt, Franklin D., 158
Ruiz, Santana, 85–86

Schlechty, Philip, 147
Schön, David, 50
school boards, 35, 159
school districts and district offices
   autonomy/coherence balance with schools, 34–35, 67–68

   branding and, 38–40
   CTE pathways and, 107–109
   district of schools versus school district, 34, 39
   funding, 44
   importance of, 158
   instructional leadership and, 52–54
   knowing student needs, 76–77
   professional learning and, 132–134
   relationship with principal, 33
   support to schools from, 68
   systems thinking and, 33–35
schools
   autonomy/coherence balance with district, 34–35, 67–68
   branding of district versus school, 38–40
   CTE pathways and, 109–110
   instructional leadership, 54–56
   size of, 64
   social systems lens in, 72–73
   systems thinking and, 31–32
school systems. *See* systems thinking
secondary education, factory model of, 2
self-actualization, 117
selfhood, 117. *See also* student voice and purpose
Senge, Peter M.
   creative tension and, 17, 48
   individual and organizational learning, 46–47
   leverage principle, 41
   reality, 45
   systems thinking and, 29, 37
sense of community, 72–73
Shuster, Grant, 136
Silent Spring (Carson), 80
silos, 33
single-loop learning, 50, 57
six Cs, 81
social capital, 32, 101. *See also* mentorship and internships
social-emotional learning (SEL). *See* mindfulness; twenty-first-century skills
social media, 119
social systems, 29–30. *See also* systems thinking

standardized testing
    benefit by focusing away from, 81–87
    calling not found in, 156
    focus on classroom processes rather than test itself, 80–87
    negative impacts from, 35–36, 119–120
    purposeful life and, 8, 12
status quo
    change and, 48, 142–143, 158
    single- versus double-loop learning, 50–51, 57
    student voice and purpose and, 44
stressor mitigation, 71–72, 119, 123
structural inequality, schools as source of, 2
student motivation, 70–73
student stories
    adapting CPSF and, 67–68, 71
    demographics of AUHSD, 62–70
    hygiene factors and, 71–72, 73
    reflection on, 78
student voice and purpose
    Capstone projects and, 111–114
    career pathways and, 22
    college success and, 86
    CPSF and, 23–24
    dual-enrollment programs and, 88
    importance of, 160
    mental health and, 120
    sense of community and, 73
    status quo change for, 44
Suatoni, Sarah, 121
superintendents, politics and, 159
Switzer, Mike, 111–112
systems thinking
    overview of, 27–29, 40–41
    community level, 35–38
    district level, 33–35
    human relations and, 41–44
    instructional leadership, 52–56
    leadership and, 157–158
    organizational learning and, 45–52
    parts of, 30
    reflection on, 58–59
    school sites level, 31–32
    template for, 59
    three-level chess analogy for, 30–37, 40–41

Tait, Tom, 42–43
teacher leaders (influencers), 56, 108, 135–136. *See also* curriculum specialists; 5Cs coaches
technical skills
    college success and, 86
    CPSF and, 21–23
    twenty-first century skills and, 24, 75–76, 117–118
Teranishi, Robert, 72
testing. *See* standardized testing
textbook adoption process, 51
three-level chess analogy, 30–37, 40–41, 106–110
transitions, 11. *See also* career pathways
trim tabs
    change and, 41–44
    educators as, 42, 54, 149
    feedback and influence loops and, 47–48
    textbook adoption process as, 51
tuition increases, 9
twenty-first-century skills
    Capstone projects for, 114
    cognitive development intertwined with, 29
    college success and, 86
    CPSF and, 19–21
    importance of, 112–114
    mindfulness, 117–126
    reflection on, 127
    technical skills and, 24, 75–76, 117–118

uncertainty, 152–153
unfreezing for change, 48–49
unions, 159–160
university admission and enrollment, 84–87
Unlimited You tagline creation, 39–40
US Army War College, 152

vision
    5Cs and, 20–21
    of AUHSD, 15–18
    branding and, 38–40
    change to achieve, 28–29, 150–151
    communicating of, 37–40
    creative tension and, 45–47
vocational education, 90–91. *See also* career and technical education (CTE)

Vocational Education Act funding, 138
voice. *See* student voice and purpose
volatile, uncertain, complex, and ambiguous (VUCA), 152–153

War College, 152
We, It, and I schema, 17–18, 45–47
wealth gap, widening of, 9

Weisbord, Marvin R., 48–49
whole child approach, 36, 62, 74, 135
work-based learning coordinator role, 106
workforce development, 9, 28. *See also* career pathways
workforce malaise, 153–156
Wren, Christopher, 155
Writing Journey, 139–141